THE PSYCHOLOGY OF SOCIAL MEDIA

Are we really being ourselves on social media? Can we benefit from connecting with people we barely know online? Why do some people overshare on social networking sites?

The Psychology of Social Media explores how so much of our everyday lives is played out online, and how this can impact our identity, wellbeing and relationships. It looks at how our online profiles, connections, status updates and sharing of photographs can be a way to express ourselves and form connections, but also highlights the pitfalls of social media including privacy issues.

From FOMO to fraping, and from subtweeting to selfies, *The Psychology of Social Media* shows how social media has developed a whole new world of communication, and for better or worse is likely to continue to be an essential part of how we understand our selves.

Ciarán Mc Mahon is a historian and philosopher of psychology. His research interests lie at the intersection of psychology and technology, including cybersecurity and social media. He is an occasional lecturer at the School of Psychology, University College Dublin and a regular tweeter at @cjamcmahon.

THE PSYCHOLOGY OF EVERYTHING

People are fascinated by psychology, and what makes humans tick. Why do we think and behave the way we do? We've all met armchair psychologists claiming to have the answers, and people that ask if psychologists can tell what they're thinking. *The Psychology of Everything* is a series of books which debunk the popular myths and pseudo-science surrounding some of life's biggest questions.

The series explores the hidden psychological factors that drive us, from our subconscious desires and aversions, to our natural social instincts. Absorbing, informative, and always intriguing, each book is written by an expert in the field, examining how research-based knowledge compares with popular wisdom, and showing how psychology can truly enrich our understanding of modern life.

Applying a psychological lens to an array of topics and contemporary concerns – from sex, to fashion, to conspiracy theories – *The Psychology of Everything* will make you look at everything in a new way.

Titles in the series:

The Psychology of Grief
Richard Gross

The Psychology of Sex
Meg-John Barker

The Psychology of Dieting
Jane Ogden

The Psychology of Performance
Stewart T. Cotterill

The Psychology of Trust
Ken J. Rotenberg

The Psychology of Working Life
Toon W. Taris

The Psychology of Conspiracy Theories
Jan-Willem van Prooijen

The Psychology of Addiction
Jenny Svanberg

The Psychology of Fashion
Carolyn Mair

The Psychology of Gardening
Harriet Gross

The Psychology of Gender
Gary Wood

The Psychology of Climate Change
Geoffrey Beattie and Laura McGuire

The Psychology of Vampires
David Cohen

The Psychology of Chess
Fernand Gobet

The Psychology of Music
Susan Hallam

The Psychology of Weather
Trevor Harley

The Psychology of Driving
Graham J. Hole

The Psychology of Retirement
Doreen Rosenthal and Susan M. Moore

The Psychology of School Bullying
Peter Smith

The Psychology of Celebrity
Gayle Stever

The Psychology of Dog Ownership
Craig Roberts and Theresa Barlow

The Psychology of Social Media
Ciarán Mc Mahon

The Psychology of Happiness
Peter Warr

The Psychology of Politics
Barry Richards

The Psychology of the Paranormal
David Groome

For further information about this series please visit
www.thepsychologyofeverything.co.uk

THE PSYCHOLOGY OF SOCIAL MEDIA

CIARÁN MC MAHON

ROUTLEDGE
Routledge
Taylor & Francis Group
LONDON AND NEW YORK

First published 2019
by Routledge
2 Park Square, Milton Park, Abingdon, Oxon OX14 4RN

and by Routledge
52 Vanderbilt Avenue, New York, NY 10017

Routledge is an imprint of the Taylor & Francis Group, an informa business

British Library Cataloguing-in-Publication Data
A catalogue record for this book is available from the British Library

Library of Congress Cataloging-in-Publication Data
A catalog record for this book has been requested

ISBN: 978-1-138-04774-7 (hbk)
ISBN: 978-1-138-04775-4 (pbk)
ISBN: 978-1-315-17061-9 (ebk)

Typeset in Joanna
by Apex CoVantage, LLC

CONTENTS

ACKNOWLEDGEMENTS

This book would not have happened without the help of a number of people. I am deeply grateful to the support and assistance of Eleanor Reedy throughout the course of its creation. I would also like to thank her assistant Alex Howard, and her predecessor Elizabeth Rankin. Moreover, I would also like to thank Lucy Kennedy, her predecessor Michael Strang, and production editor Katie Hemmings, who introduced me to the *Psychology of Everything* series, to which I am very proud to have contributed.

It has long been an ambition of mine to be published by Routledge, and every interaction I have had with this illustrious house has been borne out that dream. From start to finish, Routledge have been exceptionally professional, wisely encouraging and deeply understanding.

I also would like to thank the four reviewers of this book's proposal, whose suggestions immeasurably improved it. Their comments were an invaluable part of this process.

I must also take this opportunity to thank everyone who uses social media: your labours have presented me with an incredible research topic. I trust this book helps you better your selves. I'd particularly like to thank my own social media connections, on Twitter and Facebook and elsewhere, who have been a priceless well of curiosity to me for many years.

Additionally, I would like to extend a sincere debt of gratitude to the designers and engineers of the services mentioned in the pages that follow: I hope reading this book will make your jobs easier.

I would also like to thank every author whom I have cited: your work has inspired me to greater depths than I ever thought possible.

I am also very grateful for the love and support of my parents, family and in-laws. Likewise, I am reminded that 'my glory was I had such friends' – thank you to you too. Finally, I have something to show you all! Thank you for your patience.

This book is dedicated to my amazing wife, Helen. I couldn't have done this without you – all of me needs all of you.

It is equally dedicated to our perfect sons, Hugh and Thomas. *Ambo pares virtute, pares et honoribus ambo.*

1

INTRODUCTION

This book is about the *psychology* of social media.[1] It's about trying to explain how so much of our everyday lives and modern culture came to be saturated with these incredibly popular and absorbing services. We're going to answer such questions as these:

- How do we express our identities in social media's rigid profiles? Why does being 'real' on social media feel like hard work? Why do some people find *fraping*[2] funny, but others don't? Can we still be ourselves in anonymous environments?
- Can we benefit from connecting with people we barely know? Which services are best for maintaining meaningful friendships? Is there a limit to the number of people we should connect with? How do we deal with being able to speak to so many people at once? And how can we avoid spreading FOMO[3] among them?
- Why do we say things in our status updates that we might not say in the 'real world'? Why do we seem to understand privacy issues, yet continue to put lots of personal information in our status updates? Would it be better if our updates faded from view over time? What does it feel like to have all your past social media updates still present, years later?

- What is the point of sharing images that disappear? Why do people share their location data with their photographs on social media? Why do people like to broadcast livestream videos of their personal lives? Can you make friends by putting lots of photographs of yourself online?
- What does it mean when someone takes a long time to reply to a private message? When is *subtweeting* a good idea? Why do people sometimes write on your profile, but other times send a message? Why do some people prefer social messaging instead of social media?

One thing that psychology and social media have in common is that many people have opinions about them. Everyone has personal experience of psychology and we all speculate about the human behaviour we observe. The same goes for social media: anyone who uses it has a theory about what they experience. Perhaps you already have some ideas about the earlier questions. Obviously, in a short book like this, it won't be possible to give comprehensive answers to them. But you are not going to read one-dimensional assessments either. Social media is simply too broad a phenomenon to be given a simplistic 👍/👎 verdict. Hence, *The Psychology of Social Media* will push back on your preconceptions and draw you further into the intricacies of studying these fascinating subjects – a concise and selective reading of the literature.

WHAT IS SOCIAL MEDIA?

This book is structured across social media's most recognisable features, namely, profiles, connections, updates, media and messaging. But while most people would know a social media service when they see it, that doesn't mean it is easy to describe.

One misperception is that 'social media' is often used interchangeably with 'social network'. In fact, a 'social network' is a concept that was around long before the advent of the internet. It refers to a group of people who know each other or are connected in some way. We all have our own social networks – our friends, families and colleagues – and these overlap and interact with other people's social networks. Technology is not a requirement of a social network – even animals have social networks, and apparently some plants do too. This term has been used in the social sciences for many years, but it more popular through the 1990s as better statistical techniques for analysing them were developed.

During this period, the internet became publicly available in the United States, and soon throughout the rest of the world. Towards the end of the millennium, a revolution in user-generated content known as 'Web 2.0' took place, meaning that websites became more interactive and user-friendly. Many services emerged which began to resemble what we see today in social media. Bulletin boards, virtual communities and online dating heralded more ways for people to go online, develop their psychology and interact with each other.

But, in most of these cases, users were restricted to connecting with people they already knew. A crucial development came when SixDegrees.com allowed its users to connect with other users whose email address they didn't have. They did this by allowing users to browse their friends' 'social networks', pick out a profile and send them a connection request.

However, it seems that internet users were not quite ready for this yet. Perhaps the idea of connecting with strangers still felt risky, and SixDegrees failed after a few years. But later, this basic idea caught on and was mimicked in many other services like Friendster and Tribe. These were the original 'social networking' services: like at a business meeting, you could 'network' with new people you didn't already know.

But by about 2010, as greater capacity for sharing photos and videos became available, the term 'social media' became more popular. Certain websites marketed themselves as being explicitly for sharing particular forms of digital media – Last.FM for sharing music online, YouTube for video and Flickr for photographs. Using the term 'social media' helped to distinguish them from websites like

Friendster, Myspace and Bebo, which were mostly concerned with social networking.

However, this distinction isn't really useful anymore. Almost every website which previously would have been classified as a social networking site now also gives its users the ability to share most forms of digital media. So nowadays, while the terms 'social networking site' or 'social networking service' are a little outdated, they essentially refer to the same actual services as 'social media'.

But sometimes you hear Twitter or LinkedIn being called a 'social network'. Why is this wrong? To put it concisely, it is incorrect because it confuses a sociological concept with a technological service. If Twitter covered the *entire* human social network, then it would be quite a service, wouldn't it? More to the point, calling Facebook *a* social network implies that everyone with an account there has a meaningful connection with every other account there. Similar to when social media services call themselves a 'community', that also stretches the credibility of the concept too far – several hundred million users too far, actually.

Moreover, is there anyone in the world whose entire social network – everyone they interact with regularly, let's say – is present on any given social media platform? I doubt that very much. As such, let's be careful to avoid over-simplification: there are important differences between a social network and a social networking service.

WHERE DID SOCIAL MEDIA COME FROM?

Many societies have had some kind of 'self-technology' which people use to try to put some kind of order on their lives. For example, in Roman times, the learned classes used books known as *hypomnēmata* to take notes, write mottos and contemplate their daily lives. These had no particular order or structure – the point was to help oneself remember things. This kind of self-technology lives on as the diary – a place where you can express your thoughts, feelings and experiences and reflect on them. But there are also more interactive and social examples of self-technology, including Roman Catholic confession and various methods of counselling and psychotherapy. All of these are forms of self-technology: techniques for ordinary people to put order in their lives in accordance with their beliefs, whatever they may be.

While social media certainly has ancestors in history, it has its own features, which are unique to its 21st-century context. One obvious difference is that it is so very *public*. That's one of the most intriguing puzzles of social media: while it is very personal, like a diary or a self-help book, it is essentially a public transmission, like television or a newspaper. This makes its psychology fascinating – but it also gives us some insight into its core values. While mission statements vary across services, most are based on a very simple philosophy: let's connect and share things with each other.

That's why I use this psychological definition: social media are online services which encourage their users to digitise and publicly share previously private personal information. Related technologies like email, electronic mailing lists and instant messaging simply do not encourage users quite so much to make our own personal details public.

For example, if you create an account on any social media service but refuse to put any private information there or express any opinions, you won't have much fun. Go ahead, see how long you last on Facebook without uploading a profile photo or Liking anything. All social media services broadcast a constant attempt to persuade users to reveal something of themselves. And given the ongoing popularity of these services, it would seem that, for a large part, we enjoy doing so. Social media services run on an engine whose fuel is human psychology.

WHAT DOES SOCIAL MEDIA LOOK LIKE ACROSS THE WORLD TODAY?

Social media are an intrinsically American phenomenon. But that does not mean that they have not appeared across the world in various local shapes and sizes. Sites like SixDegrees, Ryze and Friendster are generally held to be the earliest websites which allowed social networking, and all originated in the United States. But before long, their appeal spread globally. FriendsReunited was developed in the

United Kingdom, Mixi in Japan, CyWorld in South Korea, Grono.net in Poland, Taringa! in Argentina, StudiVZ in Germany, Qzone in China and many more besides. Yet the most famous services are still clearly American in origin: Facebook, YouTube, Twitter, Instagram, LinkedIn, Myspace, Snapchat and so on.

However, many local efforts are struggling to survive. Nearly every homegrown European social networking site is now out of business. Similarly, one wonders how well services like Sina Weibo would be doing if American services weren't banned from the Chinese market. Notably, as a general rule, the further one travels from the United States, the more likely the local social media service will be integrated with other largely unrelated facilities. By which I mean not merely chatrooms or instant messaging, but also gaming and shopping. For example, the Russian service VK allows music sharing, and the Chinese service WeChat lets users pay bills. As such, many of the major non-US social media services try to function more as part of a 'one-stop shop' online platform, which might explain how they have endured.

Another feature of social media services is that almost all are owned by profit-making companies of one type or another. Unlike some traditional media companies, like the British Broadcasting Corporation, none are directly state owned. And unlike some of the internet's most loved services, like Wikipedia, none are owned by non-profit or charitable organisations.

Finally, for a while in the early 2010s, it felt like a new social media site was launching every week. But that trend has faded away, and now we are largely left with the big beasts and little else. New services like Ello, Peach and Sararah burst onto the scene, but none made any lasting impact. There is a noticeable amount of sameness to social media these days.

HOW DO WE STUDY SOCIAL MEDIA?

As mentioned earlier, it is important to clarify what is meant by social media. But the other element of this book should be examined too.

When we talk about psychology, we can mean a person's mental attributes, their intelligence, emotions, attitudes and behaviour. For example, if I talk about the 'psychology of aliens' you'll have rough idea what I'm getting at, even if they don't exist.

But it can also mean the scientific study of those things. Psychology is a body of scholarly work, with scientific methodologies and clinical practices, carried out by people of various degrees of expertise.

The distinction between psychology as a topic and psychology as a science is important when discussing complex things like social media. For example, when I talk about the 'psychology of social media', am I referring to how we subjectively experience social media, or am I talking about how that experience is studied by scientific methods? The answers to the latter can naturally enlighten us about the former, but they can structure and influence it too. This is largely because of two factors – reflexivity and observability.

Unlike in chemistry, for example, the objects of psychological science can react to how they are described. A liquid doesn't care if it is recorded as 50 mL or 60 mL, but a job applicant will care if they get an IQ score of 110 or 125. Additionally, while we can pour a liquid into a graduated cylinder, the topics of psychology are much trickier to contain.

Consequently, careful study is required, and a variety of methodologies must be used to ascertain the psychology of social media. The following chapters cite studies which use standard or traditional social science research methods and also newer, more technological and computational methods. The former include surveys, experiments and focus groups, whereas the latter involve machine learning, sentiment analysis and natural language processing.

There are advantages and disadvantages to both methodologies. Surveys, experiments and focus groups are time-consuming, as they generally require people to actively participate in the study. They also rely on participants being honest about their experiences – this is known as the problem of self-reported data. In contrast, the newer methods are faster, as they use already existing social media data. To do this, they rely on connecting with the social media services using what is known as an application programming interface. Such interfaces are constructed and controlled by the social media service owners, but they do allow scholars to include vastly more participants than could ever be imagined using traditional methods.

Crucially, traditional social science research methods are supplemented with long-standing ethical practices. In contrast, in technological studies, ethical issues are still under heated debate. Issues like informed consent are particularly challenging, as users of social media seldom realise when they are participating in computational research projects.

Hence, controversies erupt frequently, which also revolve around both reflexivity and observability. It is understandable that people feel that a controversial social media study directly affects if they are regular users of the service in question. Additionally, it can be difficult to verify such controversial findings, because the most valuable data is carefully controlled by the social media services themselves.

Consequently, when we try to find reliable facts about either psychology or social media, we run into difficulties. While it might appear that there has been lots of research published on many psychological aspects of social media, this evidence basis is best characterised as broad, rather than deep. In other words, we don't yet have many findings that have been repeatedly produced by different teams of scientists using open data and mixed methods over a significant period of time. Everything is still contested here.

For example, there are hundreds of survey studies of American university students on the psychology of Facebook. Hence, while it may seem like I am focussing too much on one particular social media service – and I have tried not to – that simply reflects the reality of the make-up of the existing scientific literature. It would be nice if we had more research on other services, but we don't, so we have to extrapolate as prudently as possible.

THIS BOOK

In the chapters that follow, we are going to look at the psychological aspects of social media by breaking down their most common features. Chapter 2 looks at the psychology of *Profiles* – which I like to call 'our own private corner of the internet'. This involves discussing how we express our identities on social media and the amount of work we put into trying to appear authentic. Chapter 3 examines *Connections* – namely the friends, family and other interesting people whose accounts we link to on social media. But what do we gain from them, and how do we tell if they are paying attention to us? This is followed by Chapter 4, *Updates* – or the texts that we write on social media to keep our connections informed about whatever we happen to be thinking about at any particular time. In that light, this chapter is concerned with how we balance the immense power for publicity that social media gives us against its possible consequences for our need for privacy. After this, we move on to Chapter 5, *Media*, where we talk about interacting with photographs and videos, and how they can let us feel like we are 'present' online. In Chapter 6, *Messaging*, we discuss a less-obvious but nevertheless essential feature of social media services – the ability to send private or direct messages between users. As such, this chapter talks about how written messaging can have a very different emotional effect to face-to-face communication. Finally, the book wraps up in Chapter 7, *Values*, with some broad reflections on the psychology of social media. The last chapter also asks what it means for us to commodify our selves on social media – what do we get for giving so much of our psychology to the algorithms?

2

PROFILES

The profile page is probably the most absorbing feature of social media – certainly where we spend most of our time when we first create an account. Picking the right username, tweaking the 'About me' section, choosing a profile photograph – it's important to construct the right digital representation of your self, isn't it?

That's the beauty of social media – it allows you to create your own little corner of the internet, which you can try and decorate in the way you would like it to be seen. But while expressing yourself is something we all like to do, in a psychological sense, it's a complicated process. When you talk about yourself, are you being accurate? Are you describing the person you actually are or the person you would like to be? And on social media, it's easy to create false representations. One might even say the whole point of social media is that it lets you market a better version of your self.

Hence, the critical point of this chapter is to examine how we negotiate both the possibilities and that difficulties that these services present when we try to express our identities authentically in our social media profiles.

CASE STUDY: 'A GAY GIRL IN DAMASCUS'

In 2011, as the social media revolution was taking hold across the Western world, the Arab Spring was burning through North Africa and the Middle East. Many column inches were filled arguing over whether the latter was caused by the former, but that debate is mercifully beyond the scope of this book. Instead, we're going to look at one sad and disturbing episode in these events, and how it illuminates our study of the psychology of profiles. In this case we are talking about a blog, but with regards to a particular case which is equally insightful into social media.

For journalists, the beauty of user-generated content is that instead of having to travel to far-flung locations to interview people face-to-face, they can find them on the internet, and question them without ever having to leave the office. So, when a blog appeared[1] during the Syrian revolution, written in good English, and purportedly by a young woman living there, it proved irresistible to many media organisations. 'A gay girl in Damascus' had started in February of that year, and its author claimed to be a 35-year-old Syrian-American woman. Her name was Amina Arraf, and she was involved in anti-regime protests as the country slid into civil war.

It was a convincing story, as Amina wrote very well in American-English, explained by her upbringing in the United States, which she often referred to in childhood memories. And her narrative became ever more dramatic with her detailed reports of life in Syria during the revolution. In one memorable post, 'My father, the hero',[2] she reported waking up in the middle of the night to hear the security forces coming to take her away, and her father eloquently convincing them to relent. Such extraordinary tales led to her being profiled in reputable news outlets like *TIME*,[3] *The Guardian*,[4] *The Washington Post*[5] and even featured on the BBC's *Newsnight*[6] programme.

However, 'A gay girl in Damascus' was shortly revealed as an extraordinary hoax.[7] Perhaps because its author was getting tired of maintaining the charade, a post appeared on the blog, purportedly from Amina's cousin, stating that she had been kidnapped by the security services. By this stage, Amina was already something of a *cause célèbre* in certain quarters, but this post sent her into the stratosphere – perhaps the opposite of what the author intended to achieve. Journalists such as NPR's Andy Carvin tweeted about it[8] and activists all over the world used the #FreeAmina hashtag. This brought her story to a much wider audience, and within a few days, it became clear that Amina was not a Syrian-American lesbian blogger/activist. As people all over the world scoured her profile for clues as to where she might be, certain details didn't add up. You can imagine the uproar when one Tom MacMaster, a forty-year-old white male American postgraduate student, posted on the 'A gay girl in Damascus' blog that he had authored all of its posts. He said that he cared deeply about Middle Eastern issues but found that when he had discussed them online under his own identity, he got 'pushback'.[9] Hence MacMaster created the character of Amina, which then became, he said, 'a Hoax that got way out of hand'.[10]

So, what can we learn about the presentation of self on social media profiles? It is pretty easy to tell a convincing but false personal narrative online – for a while. Sooner or later, bigger lies about who we are become exposed. Hence, within our social media profiles there is an ongoing psychological tension: it's easy to lie, but we fear we will get found out. But there are a few other factors involved here too, such as profile fixity, self-expression and effort.

APPROXIMATELY ME

In one of the earliest studies on social networking sites, Alice Marwick[11] examined how users of Friendster, Myspace and Orkut presented themselves. Although this 2005 paper is comparatively ancient in social media terms – of those services, only Myspace is still operational – the points made in it remain insightful today.

The first issue Marwick noticed is that social networking sites have fixed profile structures. There is a section for your name, an 'About' box in which to describe yourself and a place to put a profile photograph, and so on. But these structures are largely non-negotiable so, for example, some sites will not allow you to proceed until you have uploaded a profile photograph. At the very least, you will be continually reminded that you haven't done so. Similarly, the 'About me' text box will have a character limit – you can't ramble on forever describing yourself in your social media profile.

Crucially, Marwick points out that social networking sites insist on users having a single identity. While this has varied from one service to another, requiring users to actually be themselves, usually with their real names, made a change from earlier forms of computer-mediated communication, where pseudonyms and anonymity were more common. On social media, each user must have a single account, which should accurately reflect who they are, with little deviation permitted. This 'fixity' of social media profiles presents psychological difficulties. What if I am not sure who I am? What if it is dangerous for me to say exactly who I am on the internet?

As Marwick shows, while the social networking sites may like to insist on this 'fixity' of identity, their users think otherwise. People don't always want to be themselves! Interestingly, she also noted a difference across Friendster, Myspace and Orkut in this regard. It seems that the proportion of 'Fakesters' on a site is largely down to either its customisation or its community features. In terms of customisation, this would mean a greater ability to edit your social media experience according to your own taste, and in terms of community features, this would mean things like interest groups or discussion features. Myspace, for example, allowed its users to customise their profiles with HTML code, and consequently had few fake profiles in evidence. And while Orkut had a rigid profile structure, it also had few obviously fake profiles because, Marwick argues, it had plenty of community features available.

It is interesting to consider MacMaster here. Perhaps if he had been able to find the right Orkut community to discuss Middle Eastern politics, he wouldn't have felt the need to create the Amina Arraf profile.

In contrast, Friendster allowed little customisation of its profiles and had few community features. According to Marwick, this explains why it had so many 'Fakesters' – which were not merely sarcastic spoofs, but profiles for things like places, fictional characters and celebrities. People like being able to be someone – or something – else on social media.

In the years that followed, Friendster's owners, deeply concerned by the 'Fakesters' which they believed reduced the inherent value of the website, continued to carry out mass deletions of these accounts. These purges were at least part of the reason why Friendster suffered a considerable decline in popularity in the mid-2000s and was subsequently overtaken by Facebook. Ironically, an attempt to reverse this slide in 2004 involved the use of intrinsically fake profiles – characters such as Ron Burgundy and Veronica Corningstone created to promote the 2004 movie *Anchorman*,[12] in fact.

As Friendster declined, Facebook's popularity escalated quickly. It does seem, though, that despite having fixed profile structures, Facebook's origins as a closed, university-centric community meant that it did not find it as difficult to enforce real-identity policies. That doesn't mean, though, that its users found it easy to express themselves.

In a 2008 paper on Facebook, Zhao, Grasmuck and Martin[13] performed a content analysis of its users' profiles. Zhao and co-workers recorded details of a random selection of Facebook profiles to try and understand how social media users constructed their identities there. They hypothesised that, unlike older, pseudonymous services like bulletin boards where users spent lots of time describing themselves, in these real-name services, users would express themselves differently.

On Facebook, users are free to express themselves in some detail in the 'About me' section of their profiles. Strikingly, of the profiles that Zhao *et al*. analysed, less than 8% filled this out, and most only wrote a sentence or two. It would seem that people don't like explicitly talking about themselves on social media. Perhaps Facebook users fear that the more they write about themselves, the more likely they are to drift into fictitious Amina Arraf territory – and be found out as a fraud?

If this is the case, then how do social media users articulate who they are? Zhao and colleagues' conclusion was that Facebook users 'show rather than tell' to construct their identities on Facebook. This means that they implicitly constructed their identities through their profile photographs, links posted on Walls and groups for hobbies and interests and other indirect ways.

As an aside, this study was carried out before Facebook's famous 'Like' button was invented – but you can see why it took off. 'Liking' allows Facebook users to express an opinion without having to literally type it out.

Moreover, note how this corresponds with what Marwick argued earlier about social networks' 'fixity'. Facebook's profiles are rigid, and consequently users slip out of them to express their identities.

Finally, Zhao and co-workers conclude that this study shows that a person's identity is not necessarily something entirely of their very own. Rather it varies from one social context to another and hence will be expressed differently online to offline and between social media services. Hence, being authentic in our social media profiles requires some careful effort.

This is a point to consider when we look at other services. In a 2016 study of Finnish users of Last.FM and Facebook, Uski and Lampinen[14] examined the authenticity problem – what they call 'profile work'. In this qualitative study, researchers asked users of both sites about how they presented themselves on their social media profiles.

While Last.FM is primarily a music website, it also has some social media features. In particular, how its profile posting feature is unusually interesting. That is, on Facebook, as with most social media, users must actively share content to their profiles. But Last.FM has an automated sharing feature so that whatever music you listen to there is instantly posted to your profile. Once the track plays, all your connections will be able to see what you have been listening to. Naturally, as Uski and Lampinen found in their focus groups, this creates a whole new set of problems for those who take their music seriously. What if you are a hipster, but occasionally like to stick on a bit of ABBA?

One participant was particularly revealing when it came to the amount of 'profile work' he performed. He sometimes preferred to listen to music on vinyl records, but this experience would obviously not be linked to his Last.FM account. To overcome this, when playing vinyl records, he would make sure that he was playing the same music on his computer (with the volume turned down) so that his Last.FM profile would be updated as a result, just so his friends could see what he was listening to *at all times*.

Hence the authors of this study note an awkward conundrum of being on social media. Portraying a 'real' account of yourself in your profile often requires so much extra work that it seems inauthentic. Is this what undid 'A gay girl in Damascus' – was it too much work to keep up the illusion? But for the rest of us, might this apply too? Do we have to 'fake ourselves into being real' on social media?

This leads us to one of the more perplexing phenomena in the psychology of social media: the "privacy paradox".[15] In an analytical paper, written just as the social media revolution was taking off, Barnes noted how a new social norm had developed. While most people claimed to understand privacy issues, at the same time, lots of personal information was being posted on social media profiles. Barnes discussed this paradox in the context of teenagers being surprised when their parents found what they had been doing online, but it clearly has much wider applicability. In trying to maintain an authentically cool profile on Last.FM, have users forgotten about how much personal information they're sharing online? And this applies to Facebook users too – uploading lots of personal information to show rather than tell their identities.

This quirk of the psychology of social media is one which we will be returning to in the coming chapters. The privacy paradox is fundamentally one of the major sources of tension between our personal, individual psychology, and how it interacts with the much more social and public phenomenon that is social media.

BEYOND PROFILES

When we take the issues of profile fixity, self-expression and effort on board, it's easy to understand why social media users might want to circumvent them entirely. This is where both temporary or disposable profiles come in and also anonymous services with no profiles at all.

Let's first take a look at Alex Leavitt's 2015[16] paper on 'throwaway accounts'. This research looked at Reddit, which is a US-based news aggregator with lots of social media features. Leavitt's study included a web crawl which searched for and collected mentions of the word 'throwaway' on Reddit, in order to be able to describe the phenomenon there.

Leavitt found that people posting under 'throwaway' accounts tended to emphasise why they were not posting under their usual Reddit account. For the most part this was because they were concerned about the consequences of what they were about to say being linked back to their 'real' identity. For example, people often request relationship advice under throwaway accounts, including embarrassing details. Alternatively, some throwaway accounts reveal unethical or illegal business activity by their posters' employer. Strikingly, only one result was found to be statistically significant: women were 154% more likely to use a throwaway account than men – which says something chilling about the gender politics of Reddit.

Hence, the throwaway account seems to have a cathartic function for Reddit users, allowing them to get a story off their chest without repercussion. This harks back to MacMaster posting as Amina – he didn't feel he could express his opinions on Middle Eastern politics as himself, so he created a new profile identity. It would have been preferable had he 'thrown away' that account after a single use, but I digress.

Interestingly, Leavitt notes that creating these throwaway accounts is explicitly permitted by Reddit itself.[17] Convincingly, he argues that this is a noble policy on their behalf, which other social media services would do well to consider too, given its apparent psychological benefits.

This also shows how important it is for us to be able to shape our own psychology on social media. But if we are only allowed single-identity real-name profiles, then we must feel quite violated when they are taken over by someone else.

Let's explore a qualitative study[18] on the psychology of *fraping*. This involved semi-structured interviews with 46 Scottish adults aged between 18 and 70, grouped as young adults, new parents and retirees. Moncur and colleagues were interested in the 'unauthorised alteration of information on a victim's profile page'. This phenomenon, which takes its name from a rather crass corruption of 'Facebook' and 'raping', is known to occur when a person leaves their computer or smartphone logged in or unlocked with their social media account accessible. Then, while pretending to be the victim, the 'frapist' then either posts something funny on the victim's social media profile or alters their profile in a humorous way. Despite its name, it is this essentially playful quality which distinguishes fraping from more sinister behaviours like cyberbullying, or technical intrusions like hacking.

Moncur *et al.* were interested in the social norms around this phenomenon: how social media users defined it, who engaged in it and what punishment they thought it merited. Strikingly, they found that different groups regarded fraping differently. Overall, it was only carried out and positively regarded as humorous by young people – neither the new parents nor the retirees had much time for it at all.

While it is often assumed that social media is a 'young person's thing', that isn't what we should really take from this study. On the contrary, given that all the retirees in this study were active on social media, and even more so that some of them reportedly also operated fake accounts, it isn't a question of misunderstanding the medium, nor of not having a sense of humour either. It is instead a question of experimentation with identity, of trying out new selves. Of course, this is more acceptable at a younger age – one is supposed to know who one is by the time one starts having children.

Notably, Moncur and colleagues report what the young people regard as a good or amusing frape is one which isn't immediately apparent, and subtly made a statement about the victim's personality. In other words, a clever frape is one which convincingly experiments with the victim's identity. Perhaps this is what many of us secretly desire: for someone to take over our social media accounts, portraying us in a funnier way than we are able. Again, like Zhao *et al.* reported above – social media users don't like describing themselves explicitly. Maybe it's easier to get someone to do it for you?

Alternatively, sometimes we might want to get away from social media profiles entirely. But can we be ourselves when there is no structure, no 'About me' to write and no account to be thrown away or jeopardised? What is the psychology of anonymous services?

Surprisingly, when researchers have looked at websites such as the infamous image-sharing website 4chan, which have no profile pages at all, they have actually found complex identity processes at work.[19] Given that most other social media websites have moved to remove anonymous posting, one might assume that this is because it doesn't work. Yet it seems to work on 4chan. But how?

In an analysis of almost 6 million posts collected from 4chan over 2 weeks in 2010, Bernstein and co-workers found some interesting patterns in all this anonymous behaviour. While users of 4chan can prove that they are the are the authors of more than one post by providing what is known as the posts' 'tripcode', Bernstein *et al.* found that this behaviour was not popular on the website – in fact, only 5% of all posts contained such a detail. Instead, users of 4chan have developed a complex culture of demonstrating their identities.

For instance, one way that an anonymous poster can prove who they are is upload a photograph of themselves with a piece of paper with the time and date on it – a practice known as timestamping. Additionally, veteran users of 4chan distinguish themselves from novices through a variety of techniques. This includes not only by being fluent in the website's unique jargon, but also by being able to reproduce complicated symbols which display incorrectly if simply copied and pasted. This goes some way to supporting the earlier findings of Zhao and co-workers: because users of 4chan use no names or profiles pages, they have to find some other ways of demonstrating their identities.

Hence, as Bernstein *et al.* argue, despite having no profile pages whatsoever, 4chan is able to support an incredibly vibrant community. That fact of online community hints at the next chapter's topic – the psychology of connecting with other people on social media.

SUMMARY

Social media profiles reveal a very rich and complex psychology. But expressing our identities in them is by no means a simple process.

While the 'A gay girl in Damascus' hoax showed that an entirely fictious narrative was difficult to sustain for very long, we have also seen how hard it is to be authentic. The structure of social media profiles impact on how we express ourselves: when there is less customisation available, more 'Fakesters' appear. Yet we prefer to 'show rather than tell' who we are on Facebook, and don't like to express our identities explicitly. Profile work can be exhausting, leading us to wonder where the line is between trying too hard and actually being authentic.

As a consequence, sometimes we try to avoid using profiles on social media – 'throwaway accounts' are useful when we need to talk about something online, but don't want it to be linked to us. Similarly, it seems that we use our social media profiles to experiment with our identities, but that this is only socially acceptable in younger age groups. And yet, when we do operate anonymously, we can still find ways to show that we are members of our online communities and that we are who we say we are.

3

CONNECTIONS

After setting up their profile, users' second task after creating a social media account is probably connecting with other users. From friends to followers, social media is, for many people, largely about publicly connecting with each other.

It gives ordinary people access to potentially huge audiences –for free and at the click of few buttons. But is it all really that easy? And how real are our audiences? How much work do we have to put into building our connections – and what price do we pay to access them? The critical point is to weigh up the benefits and drawbacks of being able to connect to so many different people in one particular place.

CASE STUDY: THE ICE BUCKET CHALLENGE

The 'ice bucket challenge' is often described as one of social media's greatest successes. It began with a silly prank, but it raised a serious amount of money for a worthy cause. While it is genuinely difficult to carry out accurate historical research on social media services,[1] it seems that an ice bucket challenge existed on Facebook for some time before it became so very popular.[2] The format was there from the start – a video posted to Facebook of someone stating that they have accepted the challenge, and then getting a bucket of ice poured over their head. After some shrieking, the victim calls on some of their social media connections to do the same within 24 hours or donate to a particular charity as a forfeit.

It only became associated with the disease known as Amyotrophic Lateral Sclerosis (also known as Lou Gehrig's Disease) when Chris Kennedy, from Sarasota, Florida, was given the challenge by a friend.[3] He selected the Amyotrophic Lateral Sclerosis Association as his charity of choice and nominated a relative of his, whose partner was suffering from the disease, to take the challenge. From there it spread through his extended family and friends, but also through supporters of the ALS Association, many of whom put in a huge effort to spread the challenge through their personal networks. The Association itself reportedly began seeing an unusual surge in donations by the end of July, and before long the challenge was being issued to all manner of celebrities, including Mark Zuckerberg.

While some analysts have argued that not everyone who made a video donated, I think this misses the point. The logic of the challenges is that the people 'called out' in the video must dunk themselves within 24 hours or donate as a forfeit. If you're too busy to make a video, or afraid of ice-cold water, you can get out of it by simply opening your wallet. That's the premise of the challenge. So really, if you actually did pour a bucket of ice over yourself, you shouldn't have to donate. But, of course, that isn't what happened.

It seems that the 'feel-good' quality of videos spreading through social media connections meant that the logic of the forfeit was forgotten as the phenomenon took off. People who dunked themselves donated money, and, more than likely, lots of people who weren't challenged at all donated money too.

By the beginning of September 2014, over 17 million videos related to the ice bucket challenge had been posted to Facebook, which had apparently been viewed by more than 440 million people.[4] Of course, as the summer drew to an end, and the idea of soaking oneself in ice-cold water became less appealing, this dropped off drastically. However, the phenomenon resulted in the Amyotrophic Lateral Sclerosis Association receiving over $100 million in additional funding, which was put towards research which ultimately found a breakthrough[5] in the study of the disease. This does not include many other charities who also raised significant amounts of money. As a result, the ice bucket challenge became the blueprint for countless more 'challenges', where many other charities and causes would also seek to harness the power of social media connections.

BONDING AND BRIDGING

But outside of such cultural phenomena, what do we gain from adding people on social media, some of whom we probably don't know very well? The answer to these questions means talking about resources and support.

One of social media's most highly cited research papers was published at Michigan State University in 2007. In this study,[6] Ellison, Steinfield and Lampe were interested in how using Facebook might interact with users' psychological well-being, specifically in a concept called 'social capital'. This refers to the observation that as we know more or less people, we gain or lose valuable information and opportunities. Social scientists generally work on the basis of there being two types of social capital: bonding and bridging. The former refers to the type of resources one gains from close relationships, such as family and best friends: people who would do literally anything for you. And the latter refers to the type of things gained from casual acquaintances: people who might give you information, but probably not emotional support. As such, while bonding social capital is much more valuable than bridging, generally speaking we have fewer connections that produce the former than the latter.

The researchers asked participants several questions regarding their Facebook behaviours, such as how many Facebook friends they had and how many minutes they thought they had spent on Facebook in the last month. But they were also asked whether or not they agreed with attitude statements like 'I am proud to tell people I'm on Facebook', 'I feel out of touch when I haven't logged onto Facebook for a while' and 'I would be sorry if Facebook shut down'. Collated together, participants' responses to all these items were used as a measure of the 'intensity' of their Facebook usage.

What Ellison and colleagues found was that this 'Facebook usage intensity' was strongly associated with both creating and maintaining bridging social capital. However, it was only weakly associated with bonding social capital. So, for example, you might have met someone once a few years ago and added them on Facebook but have no real desire to ever meet them again. Then one day, they post a social media update with job advertisement you're interested in. This is the kind of resource that you wouldn't have if you didn't have that Facebook connection. But, on the other hand, with regards to creating deeper, more meaningful relationships, this paper doesn't show that being connected on Facebook is much use.

So, to go back to the ice bucket challenge – you probably won't call out someone with whom you only have a bridging social capital kind of relationship. You might like their video, and they might like yours, but you will probably reserve your nominations for the sort of people with whom you have a bonding social capital kind of relationship.

Interestingly, these associations were only found with regards to Facebook usage intensity – they were not found with regards to internet use. You have to be interacting with people online – for example, on social media like Facebook – to accumulate social capital. As such, it is pretty easy to see how Facebook is very useful to the type of person that Ellison and her team were surveying. It allows college students to cheaply maintain friendships with their high school friends back home, and it also allows them to connect with new classmates – all in all, a very neat psychological tool.

But is it always this simple? And have things changed since 2007? A more recent paper[7] by researchers at the University of the West of England is revealing in this regard. These researchers were also interested in social capital, but in relation to the newer social media service, Snapchat. Like Ellison and her team in 2007, in 2016 Piwek and Joinson carried out a survey of users. However, they noted that the 'transient nature' of Snapchat presents certain methodological difficulties. Bear in mind that the whole point of Snapchat is that its images are supposed to vanish once viewed by the intended recipient. So how do you study that?

Consequently, unlike in the study mentioned earlier, where participants were asked about their overall Facebook usage, in this study participants were asked to focus on the most recent Snap that they had received. In other respects, Piwek and Joinson carried out a similar study to Ellison and co-workers. It also used a college student population, and they adapted the 'Facebook intensity scale' to measure the intensity of Snapchat usage, using largely identical questions. This adaptation of measures across studies is useful as it allows us to validly compare their results.

Strikingly, in direct contrast to Ellison's Facebook study, Piwek and Johnson found that Snapchat usage was associated with bonding social capital, but less so with bridging social capital. In other words, Snapchat seems to be most useful in the context of deep and meaningful relationships, rather than casual acquaintances. The authors suggest that this is due to a number of factors. For one thing, they note that their participants reported using Snapchat to communicate with a small number of friends – certainly a far smaller number than one would expect on Facebook. For another, Piwek and Joinson also suggest that Snapchat offers a more intimate and more private conversational setting than does Facebook. Hence, once again, we can see that different social media services can offer different psychological experiences to their users in how they connect with each other.

As an aside, this study was carried out before the Snapchat 'Snapstreak' feature became popular. In the new version of Snapchat launched in March 2016,[8] if users sent each other Snaps every day, they were rewarded with a fire symbol beside their friend's name, and a number representing the amount of days they kept this interaction going. Consequently, with this sort of 'gamification' of its social media service, Snapchat encouraged the development of close friendships that would create this kind of bonding social capital. But how many people can you actually keep this level of interaction up with? Let me tell you a curious tale about groups of gorillas and the size of their skulls.

CLIQUES AND CONTEXTS

The quantity of people we connect with on social media brings us to one of the more famous concepts in evolutionary psychology. In 1992, anthropologist Robin Dunbar wrote an influential paper[9] on brain sizes in humanity's nearest relatives. The purpose of this study was to examine the possibility of a correlation between the size of primates' neocortexes and the size of their social groups. Remarkably, Dunbar showed that, indeed, primates like lemurs do have both smaller brains and smaller social groups than, for example, gorillas, who have both bigger brains and bigger social groups. This is known as the 'social brain hypothesis' and while it is not a watertight law – it isn't accurate for orangutans, for example, who seem to live in smaller groups than their brain size would imply – it stands to reason that one might extrapolate from this trend to ourselves. How big should human social groups be, given the size of our brains? According to Dunbar, the answer seems to be around 150. Admittedly this is an average, for what he termed our 'egocentric social network', but it did become henceforth known as 'Dunbar's number'.

The idea of natural human social group sizes is an interesting finding for psychology generally, but even more so for social media research, which became very interested in the 150 number. However, in later work, Dunbar showed how human networks also include a 'sympathy group' of about 15 individuals, as well as a 'support clique' of five individuals. The larger group is defined as the sort of people you would describe as close friends, who you would contact at least once a month, whereas the smaller group are those who you would rely on for emotional support. So it is a simplification to talk about 'Dunbar's number' on social media connections, as if there is only one – there are two more that we should be looking for too.

The core issue here is how our apparent neurological limits are improved by the affordances of social media. Does social media allow us to be more time-efficient with our connections? Recently, Dunbar has tackled this issue head on in a 2016 paper with two surveys of several thousand UK adults.[10]

Dunbar did indeed find that most of his participant's personal social networks contained roughly 150 individuals, and, within that, many did indeed have a sympathy group of about 15 individuals, as well as a support clique of about five. But what is rather striking is that these numbers were largely unaffected by how many social media connections participants had. In other words, connecting with lots of people did not help social media users gain more close friendships – the sympathy groups and support cliques stayed roughly the same size.

As such, Dunbar shows that, despite the fact that social media makes it easier to connect with lots of people, that doesn't mean we can therefore gain more emotional support. Meaningfully connecting with people still takes time.

Notably, while there doesn't seem to be much research combining the 'social capital' concept mentioned previously with Dunbar's numbers, these findings do seem to make sense together: social media may help you increase the quantity of your connections, but not necessarily the quality. One last thing that Dunbar points out is worth noting here. Social media services allow us to gather our connections in the one place, but they don't generally let us organise them into a hierarchy of importance of the kind he is interested in.

But perhaps we might not want to do that publicly. In bygone days on Myspace, users agonised over which of their connections to put in their 'Top 8' group of people they wanted to visibly list on their profile as friends. That leads us to another aspect of connecting with lots of people on social media. Psychology is not only interested in how we cope with this *neurologically*, but also how we manage it *socially*.

A potential drawback of social media is that users might want to segment their connections into different groups. For example, you may not have any problem with being connected to your boss on LinkedIn but might feel differently if they sent you a Facebook Friend request. Keeping walls between our social media connections like this is a fairly normal desire, but it is a pretty difficult one to achieve. In practice, these walls don't hold, because, as Marwick and boyd say, 'context collapse' occurs between them.[11]

Their 2010 paper involved an interesting methodology: asking Twitter users, on Twitter, about who their tweets were written for. That's a critical problem with communicating on social media: despite having lots of connections, we don't really have much certainty about who is paying attention to us at any given time. As such, Marwick and boyd use the concept of the *imagined audience*. Even in everyday conversations, we cannot be exactly sure of how our message will be relayed, or who is listening in on us, but this issue is intensified on social media. When you think about how many of your Twitter followers might be online, who they might retweet to, and under what searches you might appear in, you really have difficulty in imagining who is actually reading your tweets.

Marwick and boyd's survey participants gave some interesting answers to questions about who they were tweeting for. Harking back to Chapter 2 and our talk about identities, it is interesting that several participants stated that their tweets were written for an audience that you might not have considered: they said they were writing for themselves. As Marwick and boyd put it, "consciously speaking to an audience is perceived as inauthentic". Perhaps this was more of a feature of Twitter in 2010, but it is still curious that the first person some social media users trying to connect with is themselves.

Other Twitter users, especially those with large numbers of followers, thought about their audience in terms of fans, as a community, as broadcasting or as consistent political messaging. But even in those contexts, and also users with fewer followers, a common theme emerged: not being able to segment audiences and hence having to aim for a 'lowest common denominator' sort of message – safe, bland and inoffensive.

Marwick and boyd interpreted their survey responses as reflecting either one of two tactics to negotiate these problems. On one hand, some Twitter users simply avoided discussing certain topics altogether – they self-censored for fear of possibly insulting some of their followers. And on the other hand, some Twitter users try to balance their more professional tweets with updates with more personal information. In other words, Twitter users try to avoid annoying their imagined audiences by appearing more human and more relatable. This latter tactic is interesting as it harks back, yet again, to the ongoing difficulty we have on social media in trying to appear authentic. Hence, what Marwick and boyd's paper shows is that while we know that social media services, such as Twitter, create many new opportunities for connection, they also create new tensions and indeed, conflicts.

CONNECTIONS AND CONFLICT

Reflecting on our social media connections as a whole, it is interesting to think about the inter-relationships between them. Besides being our own friends, some of our connections may be connected to each other, some may harass us and some may stay quiet altogether. What do we know about the psychology of them?

For example, when talking about social media in the context of children and parenting, a common fear is the risk of cyberbullying. While previous research focussed on individual and psychological factors associated with this type of aggression, few have examined more social and structural factors. In other words, can we explain why someone is a cyberbully entirely because of their personality, age or gender, or should we also examine their position within the cliques and friendship groups of their school? In that light, a study[12] on how aggressive schoolchildren have unique positions within their social networks is worth teasing out. This paper is noteworthy as it demonstrates the importance of a distinction made in Chapter 1. Because they were interested in social networks *per se*, and in actual fact did not explicitly treat any online services, you could argue that I should not include it in a book on social media at all! But it is very revealing of how little we understand of the psychology of social media connections.

In this study, Festl and Quandt carried out what might be termed a fairly standard social science methodology in an educational context – they gave German high school students a questionnaire to fill in. Like many such research projects, they asked participants questions about their individual characteristics, such as their age, gender, personality traits, how much they used computers and whether or not they were involved in cyberbullying. More unusually, they also asked structural questions, such as asking students to list their best friends. This information allowed the researchers to understand the social network of the school, revealing cliques of friendships, relative levels of popularity and reciprocal relationships. In other words, some students were on a lot more best friends lists than others were.

More crucially, this structural data revealed many interesting findings with regard to cyberbullying. Beyond the individual factors, such as female adolescents being more likely to be the victims of cyberbullying than males, the structural factors revealed some unexpected findings. While both perpetrators and victims of cyberbullying were found to be, in general, less popular than their fellow classmates, this did not hold true for another important category. Those students who had experienced both being the perpetrator and as well as the victim of cyberbullying were highly popular among their classmates. In other words, children who had been a cyberbully, but had also suffered cyberbullying themselves, were more popular than children who had only been cyberbullies, or only been victims.

Fascinatingly, Festl and Quandt also say that, while not statistically significant, it seems that these 'perpetrator/victims' showed a curious pattern of connection within the social network as a whole. A visual representation of the participants' structural relationships revealed that perpetrator/victims were often found to be links between different cliques, rather than central to any clique. This position seems to give them a certain amount of influence over distinct groups, but also vulnerable to being attacked by either. As such, when we examined how aggression like cyberbullying occurs online, it seems that we have a lot yet to learn about the psychology of social media connections. Festl and Quandt conclude rather bluntly that, without taking these kinds of structural factors into account, explanations for online aggression like cyberbullying will remain insufficient.

However, this is in reference to social connections where there is some level of actual interaction. You would be forgiven for thinking that there is nothing interesting happening in our social media connections where there are is no interaction at all. But there is, and the research here is quite revealing of the psychology of these services: welcome to the wonderful world of FOMO. An early paper on this topic by Przybylski and colleagues continues to set the agenda here, as it developed a questionnaire to measure 'fear of missing out', and tested it over three studies.[13] The final version of this scale included such items as "When I go on vacation, I continue to keep tabs on what my friends are doing". Przybylski and colleagues were interested in understanding how fear of missing out correlated with other psychological issues, namely its motivational, emotional and behavioural associations. What they found was that FOMO is primarily experienced by young people, and by young men more than young women. It is also associated with not being psychologically satisfied in a number of areas, including personal autonomy, relatedness and competence. In other words, if you feel like you lack independence, closeness to other people and general capability, you are probably at risk of experiencing FOMO when you go on social media. Again, doesn't this strike you as being similar to the deeper challenge of social media: the struggle to be authentic?

Hence, it would probably be a good idea to think twice before we post content on social media – even if it is positive or jolly, we have no idea how it may make our connections feel. In particular, those people who are struggling to find their place in the world may find our apparently perfect lives difficult to stomach. But we will be talking more about updates in the next chapter.

SUMMARY

In this chapter we saw how social media connections can be valuable, though not in the most straightforward manner. While the ice bucket challenge supports the core social media value that connecting with people is a good thing, in personal circumstances, things are more complex. We saw that Facebook helped college students create and maintain connections with acquaintances – but wasn't much help for closer relationships. Yet the opposite was true with Snapchat, which is better for maintaining close friendships than associates. You have to pick your social media service to suit your relationships.

Regarding our connections as a whole, we discussed 'Dunbar's number', which suggested a neurological limit to the size of our social groups. Not only was it reflected in our social media connections, but so were the sympathy group and the support clique – indicating that we are only able to emotionally connect with a certain number of people, whether online or not.

Furthermore, we have the issue of context collapse – not wanting everyone to see every update we post, but having no idea who is paying attention. So we only share updates that won't offend anyone, or balance with personal revelations, in order to appear more relatable to our 'imagined audience'.

We also considered the friction that can occur between our connections. Notably, perpetrators and victims of cyberbullying do not seem to be popular within their schoolyard social networks, but perpetrator/victims seem to be particularly socially influential. Finally, we muse about that quiet spot in our social media connections, those people who do not interact, and how we might try to avoid giving them the 'fear of missing out', by being careful about what we put in our updates.

4

UPDATES

Until now we have covered what one might call foundational aspects of social media. Setting up a profile and connecting with others are the sort of things you do when you first create your account. In this chapter we turn to more habitual behaviour on social media. From blog posts to tweets and status updates, the ability to create written content and share it widely is present on almost every social media service. These public texts are possibly the least subtle aspect of social networking services. But who do we want to see our updates? How effective are our privacy controls over them? And for how long do we want them to be visible for?

The critical point of this chapter is to try to find the balance between the immense power for publicity which social media brings and its possible downsides.

CASE STUDY: THE TWITTER JOKE TRIAL

While 2010 will be remembered by many in the UK as beginning with particularly cold weather, it also occupies a memorable place in social media history. On January 6th, Paul Chambers realised that the heavy snow might hamper his plans to travel to meet a woman he had been talking to online.[1] It looked like his local airport would be shut for some time. Given that he had been talking to "@CrazyColours" on Twitter, it is unsurprising that Chambers tweeted his frustration. However, his choice of words was less than optimal, and this social media update would soon echo around the world: "Crap! Robin Hood airport is closed. You've got a week and a bit to get your shit together otherwise I'm blowing the airport sky high!"[2] Obviously, this was a joke – right? Bizarrely, this in fact began the protracted episode in British legal history known as the 'Twitter joke trial'.[3]

Despite Twitter being lauded as an instantaneous publication medium, Chambers' tweet was not noticed until a few days later, when it was found accidentally by an off-duty security manager.[4] It was passed on to the police and Chambers was arrested, charged with sending a menacing message and ultimately fined £1,000 in court. However, his case was picked up by civil liberties campaigners, including celebrities and politicians, and after three appeals, Chambers' conviction was quashed. And while he lost two jobs in the process of all of this, he did end up marrying the woman he was trying to meet on that fateful January morning[5] – who presumably was his intended audience for his 'joke' all along.

Since then, there have similar instances where social media updates have produced extraordinarily unintended reactions for their authors. What psychological lessons are there from such incidents?

UPDATING IN THE DARK

An enduring and readable paper by John Suler, published in 2004,[6] will help explain the psychology of updates like this. It is concerned with the observation that people seem to say things online that they might not in 'real life'. Suler calls this phenomenon 'online disinhibition', which can have both benign or toxic consequences.

According to Suler, online disinhibition comprises six factors. Firstly, there is *dissociative anonymity*. As per Chapter 2, it is very easy to use different accounts and inaccurate details online. In other words, we might feel like we 'aren't ourselves' and therefore we can do things that our normal selves wouldn't usually do.

The second factor is *invisibility*: when online we feel we can observe what's going on, without ourselves being seen. For example, when scrolling through a news feed, we can see the updates our connections have posted – without posting any updates ourselves. More to the point, even though our activity is probably being monitored by the social media service, we have no sensation of this. We feel quite invisible.

Thirdly, there is an *asynchronicity* factor: when online, we do not really feel that we are acting in 'real time'. In other words – as anyone who has ever emailed me will readily attest – no one is obliged to reply to online communication immediately. Consequently, given this time and space to respond whenever we feel like it, we are able to think out our replies in ways that we would not be able to do if our conversations were totally synchronous or in real time. Obviously, this can make for clearer communication, but it does mean that we communicate differently online than we do face-to-face.

Fourthly, online disinhibition includes *solipsistic introjection*: we develop ideas about whoever we are interacting with online. This is particularly the case with people we haven't met before: we fill in the emotional blanks in the message they send in trying to imagine who they are. We visualise how they speak and how they act, because it is easier to communicate with a 'real' person than with plain dry text. As such, when we read social media updates there is a powerful psychological process at play in our imagination. This is clearly part of how online dating works. Before we meet someone, we build up ideas in our head about them – which may or may not be proven true on the first date!

Fifthly, online disinhibition also involves *dissociative imagination*: where we treat our online activity as a game or a fantasy. This is a deep assumption running through many assumptions about the internet: that it's not the 'real world' and doesn't really count as important as a result. Naturally, this feeling can have disastrous consequences.

A final element of online disinhibition is the *minimisation of status and authority*. In the physical world, rules and laws are hard to miss. There are yellow lines on the side of the road where you shouldn't park your car. Policemen are usually visible from some distance by virtue of their uniforms. But not so in cyberspace, where you would be forgiven for thinking that no one is in charge – and indeed the internet itself has no centralised control. Moreover, as Suler puts it, the 'traditional philosophy' of the internet is that it is a place where everyone is an equal and can share ideas and resources. While this clearly is an admirable philosophy, without clear moderation, it can give rise to social media sometimes feeling like a free-for-all.

Many of these factors can be seen in the Twitter joke trial. Mr Chambers likely felt somewhat invisible: if he had thought that his tweet would be seen by the security services, he would not have posted it. This also suggests that he had minimised the idea of any authority watching over him. We can see solipsistic introjection too: he was likely thinking about his date reading his witty tweet, but not anyone else. Additionally, there is dissociative imagination here too: his tweet suggests playfulness, not seriousness. As such, online disinhibition illuminates the complex psychology of this infamous social media update.

But for the most part, we generally don't view updates in isolation. We should also try to understand the psychology of the News Feed, where lots of updates are presented in succession. While today nearly every service today combines users' updates into such a news feed, when this feature was first introduced by Facebook in 2006, it caused huge controversy, as a study from that period explains.[7]

Previously, when a Facebook user posted an update, it simply appeared on their own page. Hence, to see new updates, users had to manually visit each of their connections' profiles, or what was then known as their Facebook Wall. The new feature combined users' individual activity into a single location, like headlines on a newspaper – hence the name, News Feed. Given how central this is to today's social media experience, you might think that Facebook users would have warmly welcomed such an innovation. As Hoadley, Xu, Lee and Rosson point out, the News Feed exposed no information that was previously private – it simply collected lots of public updates from users' Walls and displayed it in one place.

In fact, there was considerable outcry among users about the News Feed. While users seldom express anything other than anger when a social media service changes its design, in this case the uproar was significantly louder than normal. Hoadley and co-workers surveyed Facebook users in the aftermath of this change and found some very revealing details about why this happened.

A majority of respondents disapproved of the News Feed, with 29% saying they felt 'very negative' about it. Most said that their feelings were legitimate due to these changes, and not because they got caught up in the media hysteria. But why?

Hoadley and colleagues answer this question by providing empirical support for what might well be ancient wisdom: it's not about control, it's about *perceived* control. When asked, 66% of respondents agreed with the statement: "The same information was available before, but became easier to get afterwards". In effect, Facebook users had felt like they had some control over who saw their status updates. But that control evaporated once the News Feed made them all very easy to find.

Again, this links back to what we spoke about in Chapter 3. At its heart, the News Feed controversy is about context collapse: users trying to control who sees their updates. It also corresponds with what we saw in Chapter 1 – at the root of much of social media activity is the personal struggle in maintaining control over how our identity is represented online. Yet again, when we talk about the psychology of updates, we are also talking about the privacy paradox.

ICEBERGS AND INVISIBILITY

Another paper[8] published in the same era as Hoadley was carried out by Debatin, Lovejoy, Horn and Hughes, and focusses on this issue in particular. Why is it that social media users seem to understand privacy issues, yet continue to upload lots of private information in their status updates? While this is another study of Facebook with US college student participants, it is very helpful, not only for its findings, but for the metaphor it uses in explaining them.

Debatin and colleagues were writing not only in the context of the News Feed controversy, but also several other privacy-related issues, including third-party usage, data-mining and targeted advertising. (Yes, these were all big issues on Facebook over a decade ago!) This paper set out to understand how users understand and react to these privacy issues.

The researchers firstly clarified whether or not Facebook users actually understood privacy on social media. Contrary to expectations, a large majority did and had made restrictions – so that, for example, only their Friends could see their profiles. However, over 90% of participants used their full real name, gender, date of birth and hometown on their profile. A similar percentage also included profile photos of themselves, as well as pictures of their friends and families. Put this alongside the fact that only 52% said they only accepted Friend requests from people that they personally knew, and you can see that there is something of a problem here.

As Debatin *et al.* delicately put it, there is something of a contradiction between saying that you understand privacy issues yet at the same time uploading significant amounts of personal information and sharing it with lots of people. How is this apparent contradiction resolved?

One explanation the authors give is that this may be due to a third-person effect: in other words, we perceive risks as more likely to affect other people than ourselves. But Debatin and colleagues are not entirely satisfied with this account. They also toy with the idea that young people find maintaining communication via technology like social media to be so essential to their lives that any privacy risk is worth it, but this too seems inadequate.

The explanation that Debatin and co-workers return to is a simple illustration, which they call the Facebook 'Iceberg Model'. The visible part of an iceberg, they say, is like the fun part of social media, where users spend their time, having fun, browsing and posting status updates. But below the water, the part of the iceberg that we can't see, lies the more substantial aspects of social media – all of our social media data, profile information, interactions and status updates, but aggregated and refined for advertising purposes.

Debatin *et al.* surmise that for commercial exploitation of social media to be successful, it must use the invisible part of the iceberg, though silently and unobtrusively. Hence, when we tinker with our privacy settings, such as hiding our profile from everyone except Friends, we are really only interacting with the visible part of the iceberg. No matter how many privacy settings you turn on, you are still sharing all your data with the social media service owners. This is how the privacy paradox occurs: we have a sense of control over our status updates – the visible part of the iceberg – while becoming oblivious to the much more valuable and sensitive information below. It is only when a social media controversy breaks in the news, almost like an iceberg calving, that we become aware of what we have shared below the waterline.

Yet this does not completely explain why we continue to post updates to its visible tip. While empirical papers are the majority in social science, it is often more useful to consider these issues with a theoretical approach. One paper I find myself turning to again and again in this regard was published by Taina Bucher in 2012[9] and is a case study of Facebook's News Feed. Bucher identifies an issue at the core of the psychology of social media updates: the problem of visibility. We want our social media posts to be *seen*, but we are never quite sure how many people do.

To do this, Bucher contrasts the News Feed algorithm with surveillance under totalitarian societies. Under a dictatorship or absolute monarchy, people tend behave in conformity with the ruling ideology because they assume that they are being constantly watched – a theory known as Panopticism. This is how its ideology is followed: not necessarily because it is forcibly taught to the subjects, but rather because they assume that they are under constant surveillance, so they follow it as a matter of routine.

While this might seem far removed from most of our daily lives, Bucher explains how it is a useful analogy for what happens when we post status updates on Facebook, albeit with some crucial differences. Her analysis begins with yet another Facebook controversy regarding the News Feed (yes, there have been more than one!). On this occasion there was a public outcry when Facebook modified this feature. Originally, the News Feed displayed status updates in chronological order with the most recent content at the top. However, in September 2011, this quietly changed. Now Facebook would decide which updates were most important to you and put those at the top of your News Feed instead.

As an aside, several other social media services such as Instagram,[10] LinkedIn[11] and Twitter[12] have since also introduced algorithmic or non-chronological timelines. Therefore, much of Bucher's analysis can be applied to those services too. In all of these cases, the algorithms are proprietary and secret, but, as she explains, we do know the major factors involved.

Firstly, Bucher notes the concept of affinity – the closer we are linked to the person who has shared the update, the more likely it is to be at the top of our feed. Secondly, there is a timeliness factor – the older the update is, the less likely the algorithm is to push it to the top of anyone's feed. And thirdly, and perhaps most obscurely, there is a weight factor – or the amount of interaction other people have had with the update. The more Likes, Shares and Comments that a status update receives, the more likely the social media algorithm is to promote it to other users.

Bucher concludes with some observations that are useful for understanding the psychology of social media status. Firstly, if you do not post updates to a social media service with an algorithmic timeline, you are effectively punished with invisibility. There's no point in simply creating a profile and connecting with people; you will not be seen on social media, unless you post an update.

Secondly, by pushing to the top of the News Feed those updates that lots of people are Liking, Commenting on and Sharing, Facebook makes it appear that this kind of behaviour is the norm. So not only does the Facebook algorithm make it clear that it wants you to post status updates by pushing updates with lots of interaction to the top of your News Feed, it also shows that it wants you to Like, Comment on and Share other status updates too. Similarly, it means that not only should you post updates, but you should post updates that get lots of Likes, Comments and Shares – so you have to think about that before you post any.

Finally, and as a consequence of this, Facebook thereby reinforces the visibility of social media updates that are already visible, and thus what is already popular becomes even more popular. It is also contrary to the type of positive news spreading that is supposed to be at the heart of social media, like the ice bucket challenge we discussed in Chapter 2. This makes it harder for less popular people to attain visibility, which also seems unfair. Hence, we continue to post lots of personal information in our updates because this is what these services encourage us to do, and they are also punishing us with invisibility if we don't.

POST FUTURE

Of course, when we post an update today, we want it to be visible *right now*. But what about in the future? There will come a time when it refers to something in the past, when we might not want it to be quite so public. Algorithms may push old updates off the top of our news feeds, but never archive or delete them – they remain searchable online indefinitely. Changing one's mind is an essential part of psychological growth, which could be frustrated by social media's fairly indelible quality. What do we know of the psychology of anachronistic status updates?

In a two-part investigation,[13] Bauer and colleagues carried out both a longitudinal study over a month, and a retrospective study looking back at the previous week and year. What they were interested in was how people viewed the privacy status of social media updates over time. Hence, in the longitudinal study, Bauer and co-workers asked participants to consider the visibility of updates they had shared to Facebook in the previous week – i.e. who they wanted to see them, from Everyone/Public, through 'Friends only', to no-one/disappear. They then asked this group similar questions about the same posts a week later and a month later. Following this, in an effort to confirm its findings, in the retrospective study Bauer and colleagues asked another sample of Facebook users to look at their updates from the previous week and from the previous year.

Overall, bar one exception, the results from both of Bauer and colleagues' studies did not really produce any striking findings. The authors seem a little surprised that, on the whole, participants did not want all their updates to fade away with time. In general, they wanted a small number of updates to become more private over time, and a small number of updates to become more visible over time. Now while Bauer *et al.* note that this is a task which social media sites do not make easy, because only a small number of updates are affected, surely it's not a big problem?

However, one finding from the longitudinal study complicates the issue. In the first week, participants were asked to predict how they felt they would want the visibility of that week's Facebook posts to change in the future. When those predictions were compared with what they actually did with the posts a month later, Bauer and colleagues found no relationship. In other words, Facebook users were poor at predicting whether or not they wanted their social media posts to remain public in the future. We have difficulty in imagining how visible or hidden we would like to become – even in as short a space of time as a few weeks. Clearly, the longer we live on social media, the more likely we are to be affected by this.

While social media still feels 'new' – perhaps because these services seem to change their design every few months – it has been around for quite some time. Some users have spent the better part of their lives on social media. How does it feel to be able to access your updates from many years ago? And how might this affect what updates we may post today?

As mentioned in Chapter 3, social media users are sensitive to 'context collapse' when posting updates as to how they will be seen by different social groups within their connections. But recently researchers have envisaged a related concept, called 'time collapse'.[14]

This refers to the observation that some social media users, when posting on social media, are sensitive as to how it might look compared to what they have said in previous updates. This is similar to the problems we encountered in Chapter 2: it is as if consistency is a requirement of authenticity. In other words, the past is no longer completely past – it has collapsed onto the present.

In this study, the researchers carried out focus groups with young adult social media users. Crucially, in a methodology which makes this study particularly strong, not only were these carried out in both Spain and Norway, but also firstly in 2009, and again in 2015.

Notably, in the 2009 interviews, Brandtzaeg and Lüders found evidence of context collapse – i.e. users expressing themselves in a happy but filtered, uncontroversial way – but none of time collapse.

But by 2015, this had changed. These interviewees expressed acute concerns about how their attempts to project a professional image on social media could easily be compromised by the digital traces of their youth. Notably, one participant, a reporter, vented jealously about her senior colleagues: "Old journalists don't have many nude photos of themselves online, do they?" Others mentioned trawling through old tweets and other social media updates, searching for anything embarrassing to delete.

Brandtzaeg and Lüders note that the effect is more pronounced on social media services which operate single-identity, real-name accounts, and where content is archived but publicly, or at least semi-publicly, still available online. In other words, this probably applies a little more to Facebook than Instagram or Twitter. They suggest that its development is due to a number of factors. Obviously, in 2009, not as many participants would have grown up with social media as would have by 2015. These individuals would have more extensive online 'life logs' than the earlier participants, and hence their 'past remained present'.

Crucially, as Brandtzaeg and Lüders report, in 2011, Facebook replaced the 'Wall' with the 'Timeline', which made it easier to find older status updates. Previously, to see a user's past updates, you had to keep pressing 'Show More Posts' at the bottom of their Wall, but the Timeline arranged them all neatly by year, month and date. This recalls Chapter 2 and the structure of profiles affecting how we express ourselves authentically. Can you imagine the amount of profile work involved in reviewing all your previous updates when the Timeline was launched?

Hence some of Brandtzaeg and Lüders' 2015 participants preferred ephemeral services like Snapchat, or private messaging like WhatsApp. Naturally, we will be discussing the psychology of sharing media in the next chapter, and messaging in the one after that.

SUMMARY

To conclude this chapter, let's remind ourselves of where we began. A British man unthinkingly tweeted a joke, not realising who would read it, and, as a result, ended up in court. This is a good example of online disinhibition, where people say things online that they might not necessarily do in a face-to-face context. In particular, Paul Chambers likely experienced minimisation of authority, but also a degree of invisibility, which is a running theme in the psychology of social media updates.

This was the case of the outcry that ensued from the introduction of the Facebook News Feed, where users did not appreciate having their status updates suddenly becoming more visible. It also gives us some insight into the privacy paradox – it hurts when it seems that we have lost control over our updates' visibility. However, our privacy settings don't really give us much control over the underwater chunk of our social media iceberg. We seem to focus most of our attention on the visible tip, where our status updates are. This likely reflects the power of algorithmic timelines like Facebook's News Feed to focus our attention. These social media features exert a disciplinary influence on users: when we post popular updates, we are rewarded with more visibility, but otherwise the threat of invisibility haunts us.

In that light, it's no surprise that we don't seem to want our all status updates to fade away as they get older – but we are not good at predicting which ones we would like to become more or less visible in the future. And it does seem that, as more and more of our lives become archived on social media, and more of our past updates remain accessible in the present, we will increasingly experience time collapse. A particularly awkward example of this is the photo of a youthful indiscretion, which we will discuss in the next chapter.

5

MEDIA

In the fifth chapter, we move into what has become for many their most habitual labour on social media: uploading photos and videos. As it has become possible to upload large amounts of data, many social media users have found sharing media to be an easier way to express themselves than writing an update. From selfies to livestreaming, there are now many ways for us to try to bring our connections closer to us and more deeply into our lives.

The critical point here is to examine the value of sharing such content: how much do we gain by putting photos and other media online, and how much do we lose?

CASE STUDY: THE 'SNAPPENING'

In October 2014 thousands of Snapchat images were leaked on the internet in an incident that became known as the 'Snappening'.[1] As this occurred shortly after a similar incident called 'The Fappening', at the time it felt like everyone's private photographs were about to become public. There are similarities to both events, given that in both cases the leaked images were private, and many were explicit. However, the Fappening mostly involved celebrities whose Apple iCloud accounts had been compromised.[2] In contrast, the victims of the Snappening were everyday folk. But crucially, it concerned Snapchat images, which clearly hadn't vanished like they were supposed to. The very magic of this service had been broken, which must have felt exceptionally upsetting to its users. It is easy to assume that such an incident is a mere salacious misfortune, but, once we examine what actually happened, it is deeply revealing of the psychology of sharing media.

In the wake of the Fappening incident, discussions on 4chan began claiming that a bigger breach was imminent.[3] This time Snapchat had been hit, and every user of the app was at risk. Shortly, a 13 Gb database of approximately 90,000 photos and 9,000 videos was posted to a viral news site. It was quickly taken down, but not before the entire tranche had been downloaded several times. Soon the images were circulating, and within a few hours Snap Inc. released a statement detailing what had occurred and who was affected.[4]

As it turned out, Snap Inc.'s servers had not been penetrated. In fact, the leak came from a third-party service: another app that could also be used to send and receive Snaps, but with additional features not available in the Snapchat app.[5] SnapSaved.com allowed users to keep images that they received, without the sender knowing. Essentially, this circumvents the whole point of Snapchat, and in a rather underhanded way.

Of course, some might say that it is a kind of rough justice that those who used such a service should suffer such a breach. And, to be frank, this kind of victim-blaming discourse is too common in the aftermath of these kind of personal information breaches – as it certainly was after the Fappening incident, where many celebrities received unfair criticism. However, it is also blatantly wrong, as the real victims here were not the people who used SnapSaved but rather those who sent photos to them. Presumably there are still many Snapchat users who are oblivious to the fact that there are photos of them floating around the internet, because someone they were Snapping with once was using SnapSaved, which then got breached.

So how did this happen? As we saw in Chapter 2, there is evidence to suggest that users of Snapchat are motivated to maintain bonding social capital with a small number of people, presumably intimate relationships too. But what happened with the Snappening incident is something different: something a bit more impulsive, and even unpleasant.

Two people connect on Snapchat on the assumption that the images they share will disappear – well, that seems reasonable. But one person surreptitiously saving the images they receive – well, that's just not fair. So why do they do it? From the magnitude of the Snappening leak, it seems like a lot of people were doing this. What is the psychology of sharing – and indeed keeping – photos and other media like this?

TRAVELLING WITHOUT MOVING

For a change, let's take the perspective of the creators, rather than the users, of the online environment. What ideas guide the designers of social media?

A classic analytical paper[6] in the history of computer-mediated communication can help us here. In 1997, Lombard, Ditton and Media argued that the concept of *presence* is "at the heart of it all". While published long before the advent of social media, this paper nevertheless has a lot to teach us – largely because the authors attempt to build a theoretical approach to understanding many emerging technologies, including virtual reality, high-definition television and video-conferencing.

According to Lombard and colleagues, presence is the illusion that occurs when a mediated experience does not feel mediated. For example, presence is necessary for virtual reality technology to be enjoyable: if you become too conscious of the headset you're wearing, or the graphics are too slow, then it doesn't work: the illusion of presence hasn't been generated. But even with the humble telephone there is an element of presence necessary too. Surely, you've seen people gesticulate while taking a call, as if the other person is standing in front of them?

For Lombard *et al.*, presence can be thought of in a number of ways, several of which can help us understand sharing photos and videos on social media. There is *social richness* – or presence being to do with intimacy and warmth when interacting with other people. There is also *realism* – or presence happens when the medium we are interacting through feels like the 'real thing'. We can also think about presence as *transportation*: so that you feel like you are actually there, or that what you are looking at is in the room with you, or, perhaps more powerfully, you are gathering together with other people.

We can see these interpretations of presence in media-sharing online. In terms of social richness, when you looking at a family member's holiday photos, don't you feel closer to them emotionally? And isn't there a fleeting sense of realism, as if you are on holiday too – indeed, as if you have been transported somewhere else? This might explain why it feels so bad when you exit the album and are unceremoniously dumped back into real life: the illusion is shattered.

Using social media to share videos and photos – and hence psychologically *travel* – is perhaps one of its core appeals to young people, especially those who lack independence. Moreover, when we think back to the Snappening, perhaps this is a motivation of using Snapchat to send intimate pictures. If the engineers of such a social media service can create a convincing presence effect, then its users may really feel like they are alone together. Hence, for romantic partners who can't travel to each other, a well-engineered dash of presence might be the next best thing. This is a factor which might not just apply to teenagers with no cars, but also celebrity couples on separate sides of the globe, as seems to have occurred in the Fappening incident.

It might also explain SnapSaved: by keeping the image that is supposed to disappear, they allow the recipient to remain in that space. Sure, it's a forbidden place that isn't supposed to exist, but if you don't want to be where you actually are, who cares? Why not linger a while in the intimate moment, and stay a while in a place you would rather be? Perhaps this is why so many users signed up for this dubious app, which resulted in such an unfortunate turn of events.

A different interpretation of travelling via social media is when we publicise not just the photograph, but also information regarding where it was taken. In a computational study,[7] over the course of a month, Manikonda, Hu and Kambhampati gathered 5,659,795 images from 369,828 Instagram users. The authors used what is known as an application programming interface (API) to directly access Instagram's data in an increasingly popular method for researchers to investigate online behaviour.

Manikonda and colleagues observe that, despite what we might assume, Instagram's social networks are quite different from comparable services. Surely millions of people sharing photographs online will produce a similar social structure? Certainly not, say Manikonda *et al.* – the data shows that they are quite distinct. For one thing, most of Instagram's connections are one-way streets. Unlike in Flickr where 68% of connections are returned, on Instagram only 15% of relationships are reciprocal. Additionally, Instagram is quite cliquish. Its clustering co-efficient is higher than Twitter's, meaning that your friends on Instagram are more likely to know each other than your friends on Twitter. Hence, Instagram isn't merely about photo sharing – it has a particular social structure that you won't find anywhere else.

Moreover, Manikonda *et al.*'s study is very informative when it comes to the banal psychology of Instagram users. Firstly, the average time between a user's posted photographs is 6.5 days. So, it takes Instagram users about a week to find an image they feel is good enough to share. Additionally, it seems that they want to let the image speak for itself, with only 41.3% of pictures attracting comment. And despite there being no limit to how long comments can be, the average comment was only 32 characters long. Is it a case of 'a picture paints a thousand words', so there is no need to elaborate any further?

However, one factor which Instagram users do seem to be keen to add to their photos is their location. Across the data examined, 18.8% of photographs shared on Instagram contain location information. As Manikonda *et al.* report, this is far higher than Twitter, where only 0.6% of photographs include location data. Furthermore, they also report that at least 28.8% of Instagram users had tagged at least one of their photos with location data, so it is reasonably widespread.

Finally, Manikonda and colleagues collated this data to produce the ten most geolocated places on Instagram in the world. Intriguingly, while many photographs are obviously tagged in areas of high population density, there is another factor at play. As places like Bangkok and San Diego are in the top ten, as well as New York and London, perhaps what we are really talking about is vacationing.

In truth, this is probably not what Lombard, Ditton and Media had in mind when they wrote about presence so many years ago. But maybe it does show that many users of Instagram do, on some level, grasp this concept. They want to bring their audience with them, wherever they go. We often think of sharing holiday photographs on social media as showing off – but perhaps the person posting them wishes you were there with them?

But you could also use social media to bring your connections into your entire life, not just your holidays. Hence, we come to the psychology of live video. In recent years, apps like Meerkat and Periscope have become increasingly popular, and an early study[8] of these services is worthy of our attention. Unlike Manikonda and colleagues, Tang, Venolia and Inkpen carried out more of a traditional social sciences study, manually coding the content of live video streams, and semi-structured interviews with people who frequently created them. This resulted in 535 Periscope and 232 Meerkat streams being analysed, and 20 livestreamers from around the world being interviewed.

The authors found that a very wide range of activities were being broadcast: everything from crafts/activities, to parties or social gatherings, to showing scenery, to live news events, to gaming and even simply chatting (which seemed to be most popular overall). Tang and co-workers suggest that the diversity of content reflects the diversity of its users, many of whom said were using livestreaming to build their 'personal brand'. Participants generally said that creating live video provided an authentic, unedited view into their lives. Harking back to the 'fixity' characteristic of social media profiles discussed in Chapter 2, Tang and colleagues remark that this unedited aspect contrasts with, say, the curated control of Facebook profiles. While the creators can direct certain elements of their videos, the unpredictability of livestreaming forced them into authentic reactions – which seems to be, once again, key to understanding the psychology of social media.

Conspicuously, both Meerkat and Periscope only allowed users to create accounts using a Twitter account. While this might seem like a restriction, for many livestreamers this integration allowed them to more deeply interact with audiences that they already had on Twitter. Moreover, many stated that visually opening their lives up to an audience was something that they enjoyed, as interacting with viewers helped shape the content of their streams. For example, participants mentioned audience reactions to their videos in terms of input to their work, such as skills in dealing with people, or ideas for a radio show or a book. Naturally, this calls to mind the concept of bridging social capital, also encountered in Chapter 2.

Additionally, Tang *et al.* notice how multiple livestreams often occur at the same event, like music concerts or sports stadiums. One participant pointed out how livestreaming benefits their connections: "Lots of people who could not be there and therefore, this is their way of actually being live and participating in an event".[9] Again, by sharing live videos via social media, it seems that livestreamers are endeavouring to engineer a presence effect: trying to transport their connections to where they are.

Finally, a warning before we move on. As Tang and colleagues mention, not only did their study take place early in the life of both of these apps, by the time it was published, one of them was dead. Meerkat and Periscope were in competition in early 2015, until a killer blow came from a much bigger social media service. Not only did Twitter acquire Periscope, but it terminated Meerkat's integration with its platform. Consequently, the deepening authenticity that Meerkat users were building with their Twitter audiences ended abruptly. Unsurprisingly, Meerkat was dead by October of the following year,[10] while Periscope is still going strong.

Such an outcome underlines how precarious it can be to construct one's identity on social media. Moreover, while the brutal impact of major market dynamics is perhaps unsurprising, similar forces can also be seen on a much smaller scale.

RHYTHM AND STEALTH

In 2010 interview study,[11] Ori Schwarz examined the now-discontinued Israeli social media service Shox. He began with a curious observation: a 16-year-old boy was constantly taking photographs, at home, at school and everywhere in between. But he only had one subject for these photographs: himself. Self-portraits, Schwarz notes, are by no means a new artistic phenomenon, but this magnitude was unusual. He hypothesised that there must be a different motive and began a careful investigation of the social context of this behaviour.

Shox users were mostly teenagers, with some young people in their 20s, and Schwarz's interviewees reflected this demographic. He stresses that only a particular segment of youth culture used this service: it doesn't seem to have been to everyone's taste, for reasons we will shortly explore.

Schwarz notes that while Shox had most common social media features, its users were mostly interested in one. Activity on this site was heavily dominated by users' publishing what we would nowadays call selfies: self-portraits, contextless and alone.

Recalling 'profile work' from Chapter 2, Schwarz remarks how much energy went into this activity. Lots of effort went into strategically posing for self-portraits and also editing and enhancing them. Crucially, Schwarz notes that these photographs must occupy a happy medium: the subject must be attractive, but not overly sexual; several participants stated that they were popular simply because they looked good. Again, there are elements of presence as mentioned above – a photograph of an attractive person might draw you in, so to speak. But it's not exactly the same, as the photos are being posted publicly – there is no privacy or intimacy here.

Recall in Chapter 3 that we spoke of how Facebook and Snapchat users maintained social capital in how they interacted with their connections. Here Schwarz notes how Shox self-portraits had many social functions. They started conversations, they maintained social relations, they verified identities and, crucially, they indicated one's social worth. As such he refers to them as a form of 'corporeal social capital'. Once uploaded, photos were commented upon in a complex system of social interaction based on an implicit ideology of celebrity and popularity. To put it succinctly, Shox was not a website where friendship requests were often declined. One user replied to around 150 comments every day which, when added to working on their own photos, meant spending 5–6 hours per day on Shox (albeit while multitasking).

But what was the point of all this labour? As Schwarz explains, the reason for developing all this corporeal social capital online was to be able to spend it offline. 'Successful' users of Shox leveraged their social media fame in 'real life' situations, like dance clubs, so as to turn strangers into 'true friends' or romantic partners.

However, because it was built on a particular ideal of physical appearance, not everyone felt comfortable playing this game. Frankly, few people were good-looking enough. More to the point, Schwarz found that even very popular users often quit, tired of repeatedly 'rebranding' themselves. In closing, he muses that those who stayed had limited other options for developing social capital. Why else would you go to such trouble? And even though Shox is dead, it is likely that on other social media services operating today, there are plenty of people playing this game of selfies and social capital.

It's probably easier to adapt media that someone else has created, and pass that off as an expression of your own psychology. You might not be able to copy someone else's selfies, but there's plenty of other content you can remix. For example, dance crazes have spread across cultures for centuries, and now surge through social media too. Like the ice bucket challenge from Chapter 3, the 'Harlem Shake' YouTube videos took off in a most bizarre explosion.

This took place in February 2013, and, in a careful study, Soha and McDowell[12] take us through its complex evolution. Firstly, they explain the 'basic bargain' of YouTube, which applies to many other social media sites too. As well as being free and easy to use, users can basically upload whatever photos or videos they like to these services and use them to broadcast themselves. Hence, while social media has attracted some professional content, most of it has been amateur. In return for being able to publicise their self-made creations, the social media companies would gather all the personal data – their interests, connections, communications – created by individual users and sell it to advertisers.

The fact that this seems like an exploitative relationship doesn't seem to have deterred amateur creators. However, as Soha and McDowell explain, this deal did not last, and the story of the 'Harlem Shake' videos shows why.

In May 2012 an electronic music producer known as Baauer released a track called 'Harlem Shake'. It did reasonably well and was even featured on BBC Radio 1's "Essential Mix". But it was several months later before it really took off. In late January 2013, a YouTuber called 'Filthy Frank', who had heard the song with some friends, decided to make a video of them dancing to it. Complete with spandex body suits, pelvic thrusts and a motorcycle helmet, the zany dance video incorporated a 19-second clip from Baauer's 'Harlem Shake' track.

Honestly, I have no idea why anyone would want to copy such a weird video. But that's exactly what happened – almost immediately, and soon, in huge numbers. Like the ice bucket challenge, the essential elements of a 'Harlem Shake' video are very simple: with the track playing in the background, one person in a mask dances solo, and then when it 'drops' to the 'do the Harlem Shake' lyric, lots of other people start dancing too. It's the clipped sample that is critical in understanding the psychology of the sharing of videos on social media.

The track takes its name from an actual dance called the 'Harlem Shake', which was popular in the 1990s – which, of course, as a shared cultural phenomenon, nobody owned. Moreover, the track itself is based heavily on samples from other pieces of music. In fact, the crucial clip that starts the YouTube videos contains two samples – one from a Puerto Rican reggaeton song from 2006, and another from a US rap group from 2001. Because so many people were involved at different points in creating the 'Harlem Shake' phenomenon, then it is hard to see who should actually profit from it.

Collectively, according to Soha and McDowell, 'Harlem Shake' videos have amassed over one *billion* views on YouTube. Throughout this frenzy, which seems to have died as quickly as it was born, the authors note that the track's creator, Baauer, was noticeably silent. But that doesn't mean he, and his record label Mad Decent, were not busy.

As Soha and Mc Dowell explain, the 'basic bargain' that YouTube began with had been quietly changed to a 'new bargain'. Because of the platform's striking openness to users uploading content, soon after it became popular it came under tremendous legal pressure to prevent copyright infringement.

YouTube's solution to this is known as Content ID. This scans every uploaded video against databases of copywritten content supplied by the entertainment industry. When an upload matches an entry in any of those databases, it automatically applies the copyright holder's preference of either blocking it, tracking its progress or monetising it (i.e. receiving between 40–50% of the revenue from ads placed on the video).

Hence, because every 'Harlem Shake' video included a clip of Baauer's track, Content ID was triggered each time. Seeing that their track was popular with amateur creators, instead of insisting that it be removed (as is their legal right), Mad Decent simply let it run, and collected their share of the advertising revenue. Soha and McDowell estimate that the 'Harlem Shake' videos could have netted Mad Decent somewhere between US$1.5 and $4.5 million.

Moreover, as they argue, this doesn't seem quite fair. Especially given that a) the track itself contains samples of other work; and b) most of the work done in making the track popular was done by a legion of YouTube video creators like Filthy Frank. Effectively, Content ID allowed Baauer and Mad Decent to harvest the economic value of the labour of every one of the amateur 'Harlem Shake' videos. But once again, like the Facebook iceberg, the mechanisms by which YouTube videos are monetised in this way is unseen to most users. Has anyone profited off any remixed media that you uploaded to a social media service? How would you know if they had? Bear in mind that Facebook has an equivalent to YouTube's Content ID, known as

Relationship Manager,[13] which similarly allows copyright holders to generate revenue when users adapt their content.

In the next chapter we will examine a feature of social media which is also hidden from public view, but that we all do get to use – private messaging.

SUMMARY

We began this chapter with the Snappening, where the horrible reality of having one's personal images shared on the internet was explored. To better understand this, we went back to the computer-mediated communication concept of presence. Engineers of electronic interfaces like social media services work hard to ensure that, when we use them, we do not notice we are online: mediated experiences should not feel mediated. As such, we mused on how viewing photos and videos on social media stimulates a sense of travel. We also saw how this helps understand the Snappening: perhaps those who used the SnapSaved conceit wanted to stay a little longer in the space that Snaps create.

We then looked at Instagram, noting its unique network structure and low level of text comments. But what is more striking is how many more of its photographs are tagged with location data, many of which are of holiday locations: perhaps Instagram users 'wish you were here'.

This theme intensified as we moved to examine the next generation of media-sharing: livestreaming video. Via Meerkat and Periscope, many social media users enjoy giving others direct insight into their personal lives. However, we also saw that developing an authentic personal brand and garnering social capital like this is precarious, as Meerkat was wiped out after Twitter bought Periscope.

Market demands were also seen during an investigation of Shox. In exploring how its users relentlessly took, edited and uploaded photos of themselves, as well as liking and praising each other's, we saw how these self-portraits functioned as a kind of 'corporeal social capital'. The attractive users of the site, perhaps with few other options for developing social capital, used copious selfies and comments to leverage new friendships. Unsurprisingly, this labour-intensive process drove many users off the site.

We also looked at collective creations like the 'Harlem Shake' videos. Here we saw that the 'new bargain' of YouTube allows amateur creators to use copyrighted material in their own productions. However, despite doing little of the labour to make them popular, it is the copyright holders who ultimately profit, likely without the knowledge of the amateur creators. So, yet again, there are unforeseen consequences to publicly sharing photos or videos on social media – a theme which leads us nicely into the next chapter.

6

MESSAGING

While much of social media is concerned with visibility, an essential element of every service is the ability to communicate privately. Sometimes we want to broadcast openly to everyone, but sometimes we want to talk one-on-one, away from the glare of the public. Consequently, this chapter, being more about back-channels, discretion and intimacy, contrasts with previous chapters. Here we are focussing on this subtler feature, usually called private messaging or direct messaging. However, perhaps a little unsurprisingly given that they are private *per se*, there are few research studies that have focussed solely on social media messages. As such, this chapter will be more interpretive than previous chapters.

The critical point is to understand how the messaging feature of social media works psychologically. Sometimes it can noticeably enrich our abilities to communicate with each other, but sometimes it can conspicuously backfire.

CASE STUDY: WEINERGATE

Let's begin with a news story from 2011. Anthony Weiner was a rising star in the US Democratic Party, serving as a congressman for New York. Happily married with a pregnant wife, and known for being hard-working, if abrasive, politician, Representative Weiner aspired to be Mayor of New York City one day.[1] Yet in June of that year he resigned his seat and has not won an election since. What happened?

Around 9 pm on Friday May 27th, a 21-year-old student named Gennette Cordova logged on to her Twitter account. She was surprised to find that she had more 'Mentions' than usual.[2] Cordova could see that she had been tagged in a post from a Twitter user she had had some direct messages from previously, namely @repweiner. In the interviews that followed, she said that she had exchanged direct messages with Weiner previously, as she was a fan of his, and after he had rewarded her tweeted support of him with a 'follow back', they had exchanged a few reasonably genial private messages.[3]

So, a public message from Weiner might not be so unusual – however, the post also contained a link to a photo-sharing website. It's worth noting here that at this point in time, Twitter was did not have a photo-sharing capacity. Lots of Twitter-linked third parties did allow this feature, however, and in this case the tweet contained a link to yet another now-defunct site known as yfrog. The irony is that, despite Twitter's reputation as being a fast communication medium, Cordova never actually saw the original photo, as Weiner had already deleted it before she logged in – all she saw were copies and screenshots. But what she saw was disturbing: a close-up of man's crotch, mercifully wearing briefs.

We can assume Weiner meant to send this privately, because the resulting furor ended his career. Many of his detractors were scrupulously following his Twitter account, and, before long, the photo was being dissected on unsympathetic news outlets.[4] Weiner's public explanations patently did not hold water. Similar to the Snappening incident, yfrog released a statement advising that its service had not been hacked.[5]

As an aside, only a few days after this scandal, Twitter launched a photo-sharing feature.[6] Would Weiner's career have lasted longer had his particular messaging needs required him to use a finicky add-on like yfrog?

However, that possibility isn't really worth considering. It soon transpired that Weiner had been sending similar messages to up to six other women, at least one of whom was underage. As such, while this case has a certain titillating quality, it is also incredibly serious. At time of this writing, Weiner is in prison after having pled guilty to charges of transferring obscene material to a minor.[7]

It is a classic case in many ways: political infidelity, clumsy use of social media, a claim of being 'hacked', as well as the disinhibiting consequences of online communication. But what we are interested in here is the intended private message. Why did Weiner think that it might be appropriate to send such a thing to a stranger on Twitter? What did he think he could achieve? Are there features of social media messaging that lead users to believe that they can communicate more effectively in this way?

PUSHING THE ENVELOPE

While 'Weinergate' is clearly another instance of online disinhibition that we discussed in Chapter 4, it is also illustrative of another cyberpsychological theory. Joseph Walther has been working on the 'hyperpersonal model of communication' theory for many years, but here we are focussing on one particular paper[8] where it was put to the test in an ingenious experiment.

In a 2007 study, Walther examined this model in relation to how people present themselves to potentially desirable or undesirable message recipients. Though this study of self-presentation doesn't mention social media, it is easy to see how its findings can be applied to that context. Walther explains how users of computer-mediated communication take advantage of its features in order to achieve their communication goals. There are four broad factors we can exploit when sending such messages.

Firstly, such messages are editable, so you can change what you have written before you hit 'send'. You check your spelling, delete jokes that don't work, add in some **bold words** if you're feeling angry, or some *italic phrases* when you want to appear profound. There are many other features of messaging which simply have no equivalent in spoken communication, each of which sends different clues to our recipients.

Secondly, calling to mind Suler's asynchronicity factor in online disinhibition, we also have a lot more time in messages than we do face-to-face. Even the fastest instant messaging conversation allows for more time. Hesitating before answering a spoken question says quite a lot – it's not known as the 'pregnant pause' for nothing. The 'Typing . . .' notification in some apps tries to mimic this, but does it really convey the same sense of urgency as dead air from a person right in front of you? This means that, among other things, awkwardness can be masked in social media messaging.

Relatedly, the third factor is physical isolation. In social media messages, we do not 'leak' what could be vital clues to communication, such as body language, tone of voice or facial expressions. Hence – in theory! – you should have more control over your emotions than if you were communicating face-to-face.

Due to this separation, the final factor is cognitive resource reallocation. What this means is that because we are not looking at the person we are talking to, we can do other things. For example, we don't have to maintain eye contact, nod along in agreement, mouth the occasional 'mm-hm' and generally give the impression we are paying attention. According to Walther's hyperpersonal model, this should free up mental processing. Hence, because the person we are messaging can't see us, we should be able to read and understand their messages faster.

In Walther's study, 54 US undergraduate students were recruited to participate in what they thought was an online discussion about the development of college course content. They were told they would participate a series of sessions of sending and receiving messages to various recipients: either a fellow student, a faculty member or a high school student. In reality, this only happened once, as these recipients did not actually exist, and participants were debriefed as soon as they had sent their first message.

Walther was interested in how different participants would use the aforementioned factors of the hyperpersonal model to present themselves in these messages. For example, would male and female students differ in how long they took to prepare a message to a senior professor?

To answer such questions, Walther recorded participants while they were composing their messages, noting things like the amount of time they spent typing, and the number times they deleted, inserted or replaced characters. The actual texts they produced were also analysed using a computer programme which counted the syllables, words and sentences in their messages. From this, various measures were calculated, including 'personalised language' from the number of personal pronouns used, and 'language complexity' from syllables-per-word and words-per-sentence.

In general, Walther found that these college student participants sent messages with more personalised language to high school students, and more complex sentences to college professors. Some interesting gender interactions were observed, including that male participants spent most time editing when writing to their opposite sex peers or high school students. In contrast, females spent most time editing when sending a message to female professors or male peers, but least for fellow female college students.

Consequently, it is clear that different people use messaging in different ways, depending on how they wish to appear to the person to whom they are writing. As Walther says, this seems to essentially depend on the level of intimacy we are trying to achieve. There is a wealth of human psychology wrapped up in the amount of time and effort we spend in how we construct our social media messages.

Without putting too fine a point on it, you can perhaps now begin to imagine how much time Congressman Weiner spent composing those infamous Twitter direct messages. But in fact, we can dig a little deeper below the surface psychology of such messages a little more.

As mentioned at the start of the chapter, published research on private messages is rare, due to the fact that they are, well, private.

However, in 2007 an extraordinary study[9] was published which analysed a whopping 362 million Facebook messages. This anonymised data was provided by that service to the authors Golder, Wilkinson and Huberman – i.e. no message *content* was analysed. Given how the global legal and ethical context has changed in the intervening years, I suspect that this study will never be repeated, though the authors did produce some fascinating analyses.

Notably, at this point, Facebook had just become available outside of US colleges, so it is questionable whether or not the study's results can still be generalised. Golder and colleagues also note that the dataset had a crucial limitation: it did not record when Facebook users connected with each other. Their dataset merely records if users were connected at the end of the data collection period. Hence, this study cannot tell us which messages came before or after the formation of a Facebook Friendship.

Nevertheless, Golder and colleagues' study is fascinating for what it reveals about the psychology of social media messages. Its main focus is the 'rhythms of social interaction' – hourly, daily, weekly and annual patterns of message sending between Facebook Friends and non-Friends. In that regard, one observation that Golder and co-workers note early in the paper is curious.

As long-time users of Facebook may recall, although it has been variously hidden and promoted over the years, the 'Poke' was once a popular feature of the site. 'Poking' another Facebook user is, according to Golder *et al.*, sending them a 'contentless' message: they simply receive a notification saying, 'user X poked you', which they are free to understand in whatever way they like. Hence, you would be forgiven for thinking that Pokes, which could be interpreted as flirting, playfulness or simply attention-grabbing, would be sent at different times to Facebook private messages, with fully typed out, less ambiguous content.

In fact, the data showed that Pokes and private messages followed similar temporal patterns. There was no particular time of the day, week, month or year that more Pokes were sent than messages, or vice-versa. Given that Pokes are essentially empty messages, could it be that it doesn't matter so much what you have said, as the fact that you have said something at all?

This recalls the hyperpersonal model mentioned earlier. While a Poke might be empty of content, it does share one vital cue with a private message: it is time-stamped. The Facebook user you've poked will not know *why* you're poking them, they will know *when* you poked them. And, like Walther's students, sending messages to either professors or high school students, wouldn't you think more or less carefully about that timestamp, depending on how much you highly you esteemed the person you're about to Poke?

As an aside, this paper also confirmed theories outlined in Chapter 2. Of the 4.2 million Facebook users in the dataset, the average number of Friends each had was 180[10] – which isn't far off 'Dunbar's number'. Moreover, of the 378 million Friend connections, only 15.1% exchanged messages. Facebook users do have plenty of Friends, but they don't seem to send private messages to many of them. This again supports the idea that while social media helps you to build a huge personal network, it doesn't make it any easier to keep up with them. There are only so many messages you can send!

To return to our main topic, though, let's examine when messages were sent. Golder and colleagues report that from Monday to Thursday message activity rose through the morning and afternoon, until a dip around dinner time, and then rose again until midnight. Fridays were like other weekdays until the afternoon, when message activity fell off entirely, and on Saturdays, messaging began slowly and remained slow all day. On Sunday, messages began later too, but picked up to almost weekday levels by the evening. In most cases, not many messages were exchanged in the 'middle of the night', between 3 and 8 am, on any day.

Golder *et al.* interpret these patterns as showing that Facebook usage is less a leisure activity than multitasking. That is, messages seem to be sent by college students during the hours when you would expect them to be on their laptops studying. Lack of activity during traditional recreation time of Friday evenings and all of Saturday supports this interpretation. Presumably the rise in activity on Sunday afternoons happens when students try to find out what coursework they were supposed to have done for Monday morning!

One final observation from Golder *et al.* is intriguing. Nearly all Facebook messages followed the same temporal pattern as mentioned earlier – for example, messages sent to Friends in other colleges were sent almost entirely during the day.

However, when messages sent to non-Friends at the same school were isolated, a significant change was observed. These peaked dramatically in the hours after midnight. In other words, college students were more likely to send late night messages to people who they weren't Friends with. Putting aside for a moment the question of what this nocturnal behaviour says about the motivation of those involved, cast your mind back to the limitations of Golder and co-worker's dataset noted earlier.

In that light, it seems that not only were the senders of post-midnight messages not Friends with whoever they were sending them to at the time they were sent, but also that they hadn't become Friends by the end of the two-year data collection period. Thus, we can conclude that sending late night messages to someone you aren't already Friends with is unlikely to result in you ever becoming Friends with them.

However, because Golder and colleagues' study simply describes the raw behavioural statistics of messages sending, we have to make some presumptions about their content. Hence, we are now going to try to get closer to users' psychological state when composing them.

In this study, Sonja Utz[11] investigated a deceptively simple question. It seems that much of Facebook content is entertaining and upbeat, so how do people actually use it to maintain personal relationships, which seems like quite a task requiring quite a different tone? As you recall from Chapter 3, maintaining social capital is a core appeal of social media. But this could be impacted by what we saw in Chapter 4, where we compete for popularity when we post updates to algorithmic timelines. How do we keep our friendships strong while trying to stay visible on the news feed?

As Utz explains, as friendships develop, people tend to share more and more personal information with each other: this is known as self-disclosure. Consequently, because that sort of content is seldom visible on status updates, Utz theorises that something else must be happening.

In this study, 151 German university students filled in a detailed survey, which began with broad questions about their Facebook usage. Similar to aforementioned studies, they next reviewed their social media accounts, where they evaluated the most recent private messages they had sent and status updates they had posted, and also their Friends' updates. Utz was interested in how participants would rate these in the light of various factors, including message content (positivity, intimacy), motivation (relationship maintenance, entertainment) and feeling of connection.

In examining participants' responses, what Utz found is both complex and revealing. As expected, the more intimate a communication was, the more participants felt connected to the sender, and this effect was strongest in private messages. In other words, we feel most connected with people on social media when we are mutually sharing personal information with them in private messages.

Moreover, while relationship maintenance was found to be participants' main overall motivation for using Facebook, it was by far the most important motive for sending private messages. As such, Utz argues that because respondents sent more private messages than they posted updates, there is a considerable 'hidden side' of Facebook usage whose psychology remains little understood. Perhaps it is in our social media messages that we can truly be ourselves.

In contrast, Utz also found that while intimate disclosures in public updates could increase feelings of closeness, this only occurred when posted by someone you were already close to. Or, in other words, chasing the News Feed algorithm probably won't improve your friendships. Again, this is an issue of context collapse: sharing to the 'whole group' rather than to the 'right person' might backfire. Perhaps we're using social media all wrong?

Of course, social media users do try to do this. Posting things publicly that are intended to be read by only one person is known as *subtweeting*. In an interesting research design, Edwards and Harris[12] examined how the senders of such indirect messages are perceived. What sort of impression do we create of ourselves when we send these?

As the authors explain, this may also depend on whether the message is positive or negative, but there is also a question of competency too – i.e. whether or not the message is an effective statement. Hence, in this study, 349 US university students completed an online experiment, first viewing alternate versions of mocked-up subtweets and then answering questions about them. Participants saw text like "Thanks to a certain person for completely making my day. People like that are awesome" (indirect and positive) but also "Thanks @RyanS for back-stabbing and completely ruining my day. You're pathetic" (direct and negative). Then they were asked questions on their impressions of the person posting the update – e.g. would they be a good friend – and if they thought it was appropriate (i.e. message competence).

The results of this study generated some interesting conclusions. Edwards and Harris' results showed that, on the whole, in comparison to direct posts, subtweets were viewed as less competent, which produced less favourable impressions of the person who posted them. So, are subtweets not a good idea then? Well, not quite.

On one hand, those who posted positive subtweets were not viewed as positively as those who simply stated the positive message explicitly. But on the other hand, negative subtweets were viewed more positively than directly negative tweets. So, you don't appear as unpleasant when you say nasty things indirectly. Hence, if you have to say something mean, say it in a roundabout way; but if you have to say something nice, be direct.

Edwards and Harris conjecture that participants preferring the negative subtweet to directly negative tweets is probably due to the disjointed audiences of social media. Again, obviously, this parallels the struggles we saw in Chapter 3 when we spoke about context collapse in social media updates: we can't see who is reading our subtweets, so we have to imagine our audiences. Perhaps we understand this when we see a mean subtweet: we understand that the person is angry but appreciate that they are trying to restrain themselves from being bluntly confrontational.

PRIVATE PARTIES

It is likely that such difficulties with social media have been part of the reason that messaging apps have risen in popularity in recent years. Services like WhatsApp share some important features with social media. For example, both allow private messaging (naturally!), the ability to share photos and videos and building lists of connections. But that's where the functional similarity ends. There are no profile pages on social messaging services, and you can't post a public update on them either. But that doesn't mean we can't learn something interesting about the psychology of social media by examining social messaging.

Let's consider why users might prefer one type of service over the other. The Chinese market for both types of services is extremely vibrant, and as such provides a good context for comparing their psychological aspects. In a series of interviews with university students, Gan and Wang[13] investigated why they liked using either social media or social messaging.

In this paper, the social messaging service in question was WeChat, an extremely popular Chinese app. By contrast, a more general approach was taken to social media, merely talking about 'microblogs' with no actual service named. In the West we would understand microblogging as referring to the effectively peerless Twitter. But in China there are many microblogs in competition with each other and have been for some time.

In trying to understand why users might prefer one or the other of these types of services, Gan and Wang took what is known as a 'uses and gratifications' approach. This led them to posit three broad reasons as to why people would prefer either social messaging or social media. Firstly, there are content reasons, like information seeking and sharing; then social reasons, such as interaction and networking; and, finally, hedonistic reasons, including entertainment and passing the time. The object of the study was to isolate where users of social media and social messaging differed in these broad preferences. That is, all the participants used both types of services: what they were being asked was how they benefited from using them.

Strikingly, according to Gan and Wang's results, both WeChat and microblogs were capable of broadly satisfying a user's information, entertainment and social needs. The critical point is how precisely those needs are fulfilled by the respective services. For using social media, participants ranked their motivations as, firstly, information seeking, then social interaction, followed by entertainment, passing time, information sharing and finally social networking. In contrast, users of social messaging ranked their motivations as follows: private social networking, convenient communication, access to high-quality information, information sharing and entertainment.

Consequently, while the broad gratifications are similar, the priorities are quite different. As Gan and Wang say, the biggest difference they observed was that social gratification was the biggest factor for the social messaging service, but that content gratification was most important for using the social media service. Notably, participants stressed *private* social networking when talking about WeChat, which gives us significant insight into social messaging's major attraction.

However, having said that, on certain occasions it does appear that people look first to social messaging apps for content gratification – that is, finding and sharing news. In an intriguing study,[14] Simon, Goldberg, Leykin and Adini give us an extraordinary account of how information spreads on WhatsApp during an emergency situation. Written in the context of a terror event in Israel, where three teenagers went missing and were later found dead, this paper used an innovative kind of detective work to study rumours about this incident.

As the authors explain, immediately after the boys were reported missing, the security services imposed a blackout on the investigation into their whereabouts. Crucially, this only applied to major media organisations who the security services continued to brief even though they would be unable to report whatever information they received.

In such a context, it is unsurprising that rumours spread like wildfire via alternative channels. Simon and colleagues report a laborious method of how they tried to capture as many rumours as possible. Firstly, they posted on Facebook seeking information from their connections about these rumours. Then they tracked each rumour from its recipient back to the sender to try to find the source of each message, following them until they reached a dead end.

Additionally, the authors also carried out an online survey to ask people how they used social media and messaging, and how they trusted them as information sources. Predictably, and in line with Gan and Wang's study, more respondents perceived the social media service Facebook as more credible than the social messaging app WhatsApp. Additionally, WhatsApp was perceived to be more private than Facebook.

From all the submissions they received, Simon and colleagues extracted 13 rumours, of which nine were found to be factually true. While that doesn't sound like a bad statistic, of the 419 people who filled in the online survey, 40% said that they had received one of the false rumours: the one that claimed that the kidnap victims were rescued. You can imagine how distressing this would be if you were closely connected to the victims, and subsequently found out it was untrue.

Simon *et al.* conclude that rumour spreading is bound to occur in any emergency situation, like a terrorist incident, and probably even more so when a media blackout has been imposed. However, they also note that several rumours were initiated by respected authorities like security officials, journalists and first responders. These individuals had access to privileged information despite the gag order and perhaps should have known better than to talk about it on WhatsApp. Once again, this calls to mind the aspect of online disinhibition mentioned in Chapter 4, and in particular the minimisation of status and authority. There is nothing on WhatsApp (or Facebook for that matter) to remind you that sharing any piece of information is illegal. Consequently, the authors advise that these professionals develop policies to deal with rumour spreading on social messaging during emergency events. However, they also recognise that such events, where individuals may come across information they think the public should know, present significant moral dilemmas. Such issues of values and valuing will be the topic of the next chapter.

SUMMARY

Before we move on, let's wrap up what we have covered already. This chapter began with Congressman Weiner's disastrous attempt to send a lewd photo via Twitter direct message. This led us to consider what it is about social media that leads people to believe that they can achieve communication goals via private messaging that they cannot otherwise. In reviewing an empirical test of the hyperpersonal model, we saw how affordances like being able to edit messages, having time to compose them and being physically isolated from their receiver might lead a social media user to try to present themselves differently than they would face-to-face.

However, we also saw that Pokes were sent at the same time as Facebook private messages, suggesting that timestamps are a crucial clue to understanding messaging on social media. And while most messages were sent at times when one would expect students to be studying, which suggests that social media is more of a multitasking than leisure activity, it did seem that messages sent late at night were unlikely to result in Friendship.

To get deeper into the psychology of these messages, we examined a study which asked Facebook users about their motivation and interpretation of private messages and status updates. While News Feeds are positive and upbeat, within private messages, users are more interested in disclosing personal information to each other. In fact, relationship maintenance is not only a major motivation for using social media, but the most important motivation for using messages.

We also looked at more destructive cases where, instead of sending a private message, we subtweet publicly. On the whole, these indirect messages are seen to produce worse impressions of the poster. However, posting a negative but indirect message was viewed more favourably than saying the same thing candidly, whereas positive messages were best when candid.

These complexities of the audiences of social media led us to contrast it with social messaging. We saw that while social media and social messaging services could generally satisfy users' content, social and hedonistic gratifications, there were noticeable differences below these broad factors. Essentially, while social messaging provided social satisfaction, social media provided content satisfaction.

Following on from that, we looked at how information seeking on social messaging can be problematic, particularly in the context of rumour spreading during emergency situations. A core problem here seems to be, once again, the minimisation of status and authority. It is difficult to be conscious of moral or legal restrictions on sharing information while sending messages in these environments.

7

VALUES

In our final chapter, we will discuss a characteristic of social media which is not as easily apparent as any we have dealt with thus far. To be clear, there are two meanings to the word 'values', and in this chapter I mean both of them. When we say 'values', we can mean numbers or digits, like your total number of Twitter followers or the days of your Snapchat streak or the timestamp on the Facebook private message you received. But values can also mean morals, or principles. Strangely, for social media, the latter very much involves the former.

Because it's not merely that users see numbers attached to every piece of social media content, but that the operators of the services do too. And it is from those numbers that important decisions are made about how the services are controlled.

In the Introduction to this book I gave a psychological definition of social media: online services which encourage their users to digitise and publicly share previously private personal information. Up till now, with perhaps the exception of the Chapter 6, we have largely focussed on the 'publicly share' bit, but now we need to look at the 'digitise' aspect: how psychology gets broken down into numbers.

However, before we consider this chapter's case study, let's review the preceding chapters, and remind ourselves of their main conclusions.

TL; DR[1]

In Chapter 1, the general shape of the book and its objects of interest were introduced. Both psychology and social media are topics which nearly everybody has an opinion on, because so many of us are intimately involved with both of them. Additionally, I stressed the limitations of the scientific literature: there is a distinct lack of solid, open and transparent science here.

In the second chapter, we looked at social media profiles and how we express our selves within them. The Amina Arraf hoax suggested that while it is possible to be completely fake on social media, it is not an illusion that can be sustained for long. Essentially, the structure of social media profiles affects the expression of our identities to a significant degree. Hence, for many of us, it is easier to 'show rather than tell' who we are, rather than explicitly claiming our identity. This is because 'profile work' can be demanding and can feel inauthentic if it involves too much effort. But putting any personal information at all in a social media profile seems to be inconsistent with the widespread concern for over how that personal information is being used: in this chapter, the privacy paradox was introduced.

In that light, the use of throwaway social media profiles doesn't seem so strange. Similarly, our ability to maintain a sense of identity and community in anonymous social media environments with no profiles at all suggests a certain degree of psychological resilience. The social media profile is a useful proving ground for constructing authentic identities, but it cannot completely contain them. It is like a kind of straitjacket that we feel comfortable wearing at the start, but might find it hard to work our way out of later on.

In the third chapter, we focussed on connections, and the complexity of their value to us. While social media's cultural power can be seen in the positive outcomes of the ice bucket challenge, everyday connections are less dazzling, but perhaps more psychologically interesting.

Some services, like Facebook, are good for creating and maintaining looser connections like acquaintances, but others, like Snapchat, are better for closer connections, like best friends. Additionally, while social media allow us to reach huge numbers of people, 'Dunbar's number' suggests that neurologically there isn't much point in connecting with more than 150, as we don't gain more close friends the more connections we add. In fact, the number of people from whom we gain emotional support and sympathy seems to be a small fraction of our total number of connections.

Moreover, the fact that we may want to present our selves differently to different groups within our connections is seldom recognised by social media services. We cannot see who is paying attention to us at any particular moment, so we have to imagine who our audience is and, as a result, aim for the lowest common denominator in our connections.

As such, context collapse is a running theme throughout the psychology of social media connections. Additionally, the interrelationships between our connections are difficult to know, as we saw with the social network effects of cyberbullying. Moreover, it is trying to get a sense of who our connections actually are that might encourage us to refrain from posting updates that could provoke 'fear of missing out' among them, especially those lacking independence and autonomy.

Following this, in the fourth chapter we focussed directly on the psychology of updates. This began with the Twitter joke trial, a classic case of online disinhibition, where social media users say things online that we might not say in the 'real world'. We saw evidence of dissociative imagination and solipsistic introjection, as Paul Chambers playfully envisaged his date reading his witty tweet. However, as we come to the close of this book, other elements of Suler's theorising seem more relevant - namely the sense of invisibility and minimised authority.

To wit, in this chapter we also explored the Facebook News Feed outcry, and what it tells us about the privacy paradox. Social media users became frustrated at their lack of control over their updates, particularly when they suddenly became more visible. This led us to a discussion of the Facebook iceberg, as we began to understand that our privacy settings only control the least valuable aspects of our data. We don't seem to consider what happens below the water line of social media, perhaps because algorithms keep our attention focussed on the Timelines, by threatening us with invisibility if we don't keep posting to them.

Yet social media has a distinctly permanent quality, as once updates fall from the top of our feeds, they still remain searchable forever. Hence it is strange that we don't seem to want all our updates to fade from view over time. We are poor at predicting what level of privacy we would like in the near future. But at the same time, it is quite clear that having a lifetime's worth of updates collapsed onto the here-and-now can be an unpleasant experience. How do we maintain enough visibility to be sociable, yet enough privacy to grow authentically?

That theme continued into the fifth chapter, where I reported on the psychology of media and the meaning of the types of images and videos we share online. Beginning with the Snappening incident, we saw how the magic of Snapchat was shattered in a rather disturbing way. We saw how this illusion, where a mediated experience does not feel mediated, is best explained by the concept of presence. This also helps us understand sharing media online as a kind of psychological travel – helping us bring our social media connections to us through the photographs and videos we share online. In that light, not only can we see why users of SnapSaved tried to stay a little longer in a forbidden space, but also why Instagram users share location data to try to bring their connections on vacation with them. Additionally, with regard to the next generation of media-sharing, we saw how livestreamers like to intensify their personal brand with their audiences by providing them with raw, unedited insight into their personal lives. But not only did we see how precarious this practice was, as a larger social media service killed off a smaller one, we also looked at the hazards of building social capital by putting lots of photographs of yourself online. Reminding us once again of profile work, the effort involved in creating and promoting these selfies seems onerous, even for the highly attractive. That brought us to the collective labour of the 'Harlem Shake' videos, which provided a useful insight into the commerce of collective memes. Here we noted that, as this phenomenon took off and a record company made a profit because the videos included a snippet of their copywritten content (which was itself a sample of other artists' work), it is likely that the amateur creators were oblivious of the wealth they had created.

In the sixth chapter, we moved on to messaging, which began with Congressman Weiner's failed attempt to send a lewd Twitter direct message. This brought us to another cyberpsychological theory, namely hyperpersonal communication, which demonstrated how different features of online messaging can be used to effect various communication goals. The fact that we can do things like edit messages and delay sending them means that we can send a variety of clues to our recipients, while at the same time preventing emotional leakage via facial expressions and vocal tone. But we can't prevent timestamps from being transmitted, and they are important to understanding messaging, especially empty messages like Pokes. Moreover, the daily patterns of sending Facebook messages showed how social media usage seems to occur when students should be studying, but also that late night messages don't produce Friendships.

But within the messages that are exchanged between Facebook Friends, we saw that when intimate disclosures occur, relationships are maintained. Moreover, it also appeared that public disclosures are unlikely to result in increased feelings of closeness. It is in the privacy of social media messages that perhaps we can truly be ourselves.

But personal conversations do sometimes spill out into the public area, and the research shows that subtweets do, on the whole, produce less favourable impressions of those who post them. Furthermore, while positive messages were best said directly, negative messages were viewed more sympathetically when stated indirectly. Probably due to the complex nature of social media audiences, perhaps there is a place for the subtweet after all.

This seems to explain some of the attraction of social messaging apps, which we found to be preferred by users for their privacy and social gratifications, whereas social media was prioritised for information. Finally, this brought us to an exploration of the spread of a rumour on WhatsApp during a security lockdown in Israel, where we encountered the moral dilemma that we might face when in an emergency. How do we evaluate when sharing information might be harmful?

CASE STUDY: HUMDOG

The use of computer-mediated communication during a tense situation leads us neatly into our final case study. Here we are going back to an era just prior to the emergence of social media: the tragic tale of Carmen Hermosillo. In 2008, she became one of the earliest known instances of an internet-related death.[2] Before she died, Hermosillo was very active on an early precursor of social media. Known as the Whole Earth 'Lectronic Link (or the WELL for short), this electronic bulletin board was established in 1985 and is still in operation today.[3] The WELL offers a number of services, such as email and personal web pages, but is best known for its discussion forums, also known as conferences. It was here, through the mid-1980s and early 1990s, that the WELL saw the earliest instances of many aspects of internet culture with which we are all now quite familiar, and this is where the very idea of a 'virtual community' originated.[4] Debates around freedom of expression and the significance of online friendships all occurred here, and were commonly accompanied by the type of 'flaming' that still characterises computer-mediated communication.[5]

Its members included several early internet pioneers like John Perry Barlow, but also Carmen Hermosillo. She was present on many other online communities, but it was her presence on the WELL that we are most interested in.

Many early electronic communities like the WELL were suffused with a kind of idealistic, if not utopian, ideology.[6] It was perhaps not often stated as explicitly as Facebook's old motto – 'Facebook helps you connect and share with the people in your life'[7] – but this generally positive mood drove the development of online communities for a long time.

Carmen Hermosillo was one of the earliest contributors to many online communities, but also one of the first to puncture this thinking. In a 1994 essay, *pandora's vox: on community in cyberspace*,[8] Hermosillo begins by stating that she assumed that interacting with people online would be the same as interacting with people anywhere else. But it didn't turn out like that.

She goes on to describe a number of disturbing incidents which had taken place on the WELL, such as when instances of apparent infidelity and familial disputes played out in its electronic conferences, exploding into days and days of emotional conversations.

Critically, she noted that what made these incidents different from the normal run of things in the WELL is that its owners decided to delete them from its record. For Hermosillo, it is this deletion which allows us to see what normally happens: highly emotional conversations actually increase traffic to the website. She argues:

> what i am getting at here is that electronic community is a commercial enterprise that dovetails nicely with the increasing trend towards dehumanization in our society: it wants to commodify human interaction, enjoy the spectacle regardless of the human cost.

In other words, in spite of the fact that the WELL had, as she put it, 'an old fashioned hippie aura' and that cyberspace was assumed to be "some kind of *island of the blessed* where people are free to indulge and express their Individuality", the reality is somewhat different: the underlying logic is commercial.

Similarly, cast your mind back to the kidnapping rumours spread on WhatsApp. When those who broke the gag order first shared information, not only was there no visible moral authority reminding them that doing so was illegal, neither did they stop to think that they were about to drive a significant amount of traffic to WhatsApp.

As such, when people engage in emotionally charged conversations in these spaces, a spectacle is created, which drives internet traffic. Hence our personal psychological difficulties are turned into something of commercial value: we commodify our selves. This is not a comfortable realisation for many people, and by all accounts Hermosillo's article caused considerable consternation in the WELL, which she distanced herself from on occasion.

Her story ended up a tragic one, and it behooves us to think carefully about her message for us. What is our *value* to social media? Notably, Hermosillo's profile is still live on LinkedIn[9] – still providing that social media service with content, despite the fact that she has been dead for over a decade.

THE DIGITAL PERSONALITY

Many aspects of the internet have changed since Hermosillo was writing, but recently, I have been reminded of the poignancy of her thoughts, as the core issue she pointed to endures, and has actually intensified. The commodification of psychology is evident all over social media, as we have seen in many places – the Last.FM user playing the same music on vinyl and on his computer so that his profile would be kept up to date, the teenagers on Shox using selfies to climb the social ladder and the Twitter users who shared personal information in their updates so as not to lose followers due to context collapse. These strike me as verging close to the kind of dehumanisation that Hermosillo railed against, but here we are interested in something subtler and more pervasive.

After the 2016 US presidential election, many post-mortem analyses focussed on the role of social media, but here I will focus on the most relevant aspect – namely, the research paper on which Cambridge Analytica was built[10] and the resultant controversy developed. In this study,[11] Kosinski, Stillwell and Graepel were interested in how a person's private attributes – such as personality traits, political beliefs and even sexuality – could be predicted by analysing their public behaviour, i.e. their social media activity. This study had over 58,000 US participants – an extraordinary number for such a study. How they achieved this is methodologically quite clever, but also exceptionally revealing of the psychology of social media.

If you have spent any time on the internet recently, you will have come across online quizzes. So much of pop culture has been parsed into this format that it's hard to remember a time before such precious content as 'What's Your Zodiac Sign's Ice Cream Flavor?'[12] and 'We Know How Many Sexual Partners You've Had Based On Your Favorite Potato Dish'.[13] People seem to love filling out these quizzes and getting silly feedback about themselves.

The genius of the Kosinski *et al.* study is that they used a similar mechanism to attract participants and hence gather data. One of the authors had created the myPersonality app on the Facebook platform, where users could fill in a personality questionnaire and get personalised feedback.[14] In comparison to most psychological research, this is unusual: you seldom get personalised results when you partake in a study. As such, the Kosinski study got lots of participants by putting a quiz on Facebook and giving them psychological feedback – which presumably was more accurate than those mentioned previously.

Now while much of this is harmless fun, it does reflect a deep yet under-examined link between social media and *psychometrics* – the subdiscipline which attempts to measure and classify psychological phenomena, such as in personality questionnaires. The idea is that if you give people a questionnaire with plenty of options, using various statistical techniques you can group them into categories according to options they select. There is a certain degree of circular reasoning here – as in, did you select the X answers because you are an X type of person? – but that has been an ongoing problem in psychometric theory for decades.

As such, correlating personality test data with other sources of information is of major interest to psychometricians, and once it became feasible to do this with social media data, it represented an intriguing opportunity. This was the next step in the study: upon taking the myPersonality quiz, participants had the option of sharing their Facebook Likes with the researchers.

In their paper, Kosinski *et al.* compared these Likes to what participants had entered into the personality quiz, which also contained demographic items and a measure of intelligence. It threw up some rather predictable results – Facebook users who Liked 'The Bible' were highly likely to be Christians and those who Liked '293 Things To Do In Class When You Are Bored' were more likely to be young.

But it was the fact that Kosinksi's study also isolated less obvious and more confidential traits that caused controversy. For example, lower intelligence was predicted by Liking 'Harley Davidson' and male homosexuality by Liking 'Kathy Griffin'. Throughout the paper, the authors stress that privacy concerns are warranted here and present serious challenges. For example, an insurance company could easily take advantage of this by targeting fans of *The Addams Family* with advertisements emphasising security benefits – as this paper revealed them as likely to be low in emotional stability and hence more susceptible to that kind of persuasion.

Controversy erupted when it later emerged that such correlations had been used in order to target political advertisements. However, this merely made explicit what had long been hidden in plain sight. All of your social media activity is being scrutinised by service owners in order to target you with more effective advertisements: again, we are looking at the underside of the Facebook iceberg.

The Kosinski study simply showed how this could be done, and Cambridge Analytica took up the challenge. In other words, a more sophisticated version of what Carmen Hermosillo warned about: psychology being commodified. Your being on social media essentially takes the form of a probability calculation: how likely it is you will click on a given ad. This is how you are *valued*.

In fact, while much attention has focussed on this study, before it was published, Facebook had already registered a patent with a similar aim – inferring personality traits from social media activity for better targeting – though it says it never used it.[15] Now while the efficacy of this methodology to actually change voters' minds is still under question,[16] it is beyond the scope of this book. What remains for us to investigate is how well this model of psychology stacks up.

Many research papers are based on the assumption, like the Kosinski study, that social media data accurately reflects 'real life'. In one particular study of the Russian social media service VK (previously known as Vkontakt), Donchenko and colleagues begin with the fairly innocuous statement that "Social networks provide a powerful reflection of the structure and dynamics of the modern society".[17] Here, the authors were interested in the concept of 'social tension', or how satisfied or dissatisfied various social groups may feel about their life and social environment in comparison with their expectations. Naturally, if citizens are not satisfied, social tension increases and hence protests could take place.

Crucially, they note that governments do not have adequate 'mechanisms of feedback' for social tension. Donchenko *et al.* cite previous work estimating social tension using economic indicators like price increases and income per capita, and of course questionnaires measuring levels of trust and dissatisfaction with public authorities. Obviously, such estimates will be slow to calculate. Hence, if social media does truly 'reflect the structure of modern society', then social tension could be automatically computed using such data.

As such, the authors searched VK data for indicators of social tension, using keywords to find discussion of things like unemployment, corruption and inflation. Strikingly, this found that social tension seemed to be little in evidence during the winter months, but spiked after March – evidently, no one protests in Russia during the coldest time of the year. But it did find that social tension was highest among young users of VK in large, wealthy cities like Moscow and St. Petersburg. This doesn't really tell us much. Donchenko and colleagues recommend further research, but it does leave one wondering: is social media data an accurate representation of real life?

DELETE YOUR ACCOUNT

This point isolates an awkward problem. There is a certain tension, if not outright contradiction, between two regularly stated 'facts' about social media. On the one hand, it can encourage us to new behaviours – like the ice bucket challenge. But on the other hand, it accurately reflects who we are, as happens in any API study, such as Kosinski's. Isn't there a contradiction there? As noted scholar of computer-mediated communication José van Dijck has put it, "Promoting the idea of metadata as traces of human behavior and of platforms as neutral facilitators seems squarely at odds with the well-known practices of data filtering and algorithmic manipulation for commercial or other reasons".[18]

How can we use the same social media services to *reflect* but also *cause* psychological phenomena? It can't be both, surely? At the very least, casting our mind back to Bucher's paper in Chapter 4, it would seem that what is popular becomes more popular on social media.

This conundrum leads us to consider the general state of social media data. It would be facile to point to recent reports of both Facebook[19] and Twitter[20] deleting millions of 'fake' accounts, so let's examine a different flaw in social media's façade. An interesting study on Chinese social media from 2012[21] can enlighten us. Reports of politically sensitive updates being deleted by government censors had circulated for some time, but Bamman, O'Connor, Smith and colleagues were the first to empirically examine the phenomenon. To do this, they carried out an analysis of Sina Weibo posts using its API to retrieve 56 million updates posted between June 27th and September 30th 2011.

Clearly, as Bamman and co-workers state, we can never know *why* a given social media update has been deleted, but they did record several extremely revealing patterns. After a short period of time had elapsed, they took a sample of 1.3 million updates and used the API to check whether or not they remained online. This revealed that 212,583 had been deleted, or more than 16 percent – not an insignificant quantity. Of those, taking care to avoid repetition and spam content, the authors noted a clear pattern of political sensitivity to the deletions. Updates which included the Chinese language characters for "Ministry of Truth", taken as an ironic reference to state propaganda, were highly likely to be deleted, as were those referring to Falun Gong, the banned spiritual group. Shockingly, the authors also estimated that as many as 53% of all updates posted in Tibet were removed, which is an extraordinary level of repression. I can barely imagine what it feels like to use social media in such a context – can you?

In the light of the Israeli study reported in Chapter 6, one observation is very interesting. Most of the deletions are clearly politically sensitive, but one pattern was less obvious, incorporating terms like 'nuclear defence' and 'salt'. The authors suggest that this refers to the Chinese government's attempts to suppress false information in the wake of the 2011 Fukushima nuclear disaster. In this case, a claim spread that people could protect themselves from radiation poisoning by using iodised salt. Hence, instead of using a gag order like the Israeli security services did, the Chinese government simply deleted the rumour from Sina Weibo. One wonders if other governments wish they could also remove rumours from the social media record too, but I digress.

What is deemed to be socially undesirable by the Chinese authorities is erased from social media: there is simply no data for it. Hence, this API study actually shows the limitations of this type of research. But, more to the point, it also shows, once again, the perils of placing one's psychology in the hands of a social media service that can delete it at will.

One might argue that such censorship only happens on Chinese social media. However, Western services have problems of a different kind, but a similar magnitude. In a recent study,[22] Mihály Héder reports on a 'black market' for upvotes on Reddit and other social media services. He was interested in the practice of microwork, where businesses can pay individuals on crowdsourcing platforms to execute small, menial tasks that they can do quickly in return for a small fee. This could mean checking that a website loads correctly or that photographs include what they are supposed to – the idea being that you could do hundreds of them over the course of a day and potentially make an honest day's wage overall.

Héder investigated one such microwork platform and recorded the content of the tasks there. Surprisingly, most of them seemed to involve various social media services, including Reddit, Instagram, Facebook, LinkedIn, Snapchat and Twitter. While a wide variety of activities were listed, the campaigns that were most common and had the biggest budgets included Liking/upvoting, commenting/posting and creating accounts on these services. For example, Héder reports that one campaign spent the princely sum of $251.90 to acquire as many as 2,290 YouTube accounts, which seems surprisingly cheap. What could you do with 2,000 social media accounts?

Noting that he was examining only one of a large number of similar crowdsourcing platforms, Héder makes some conclusions as to the efficacy of the campaigns he recorded. In terms of likes and upvotes, he surmises that the numbers involved would not make a big difference with regard to the big news stories, such as those involving political events or celebrities. However, they would certainly have an impact in smaller contexts: for example, he counted that over 77,000 upvotes had been bought on Reddit, which would have a considerable influence in any of its communities.

With regard to comments, while Héder states that it is unclear what purpose they would achieve, the fact that 60,000 of them were bought on YouTube would be enough to derail any conversation there. Similarly, with regard to online voting, he notes that all but the biggest contests could be swindled by campaigns using this kind of microworker platform. Finally, he also says that the fact that several thousand social media accounts were observed to change hands is troubling, and indeed it presents significant security risks.

Our own concerns are a little different. Recall that, in Chapter 2, we noted that Reddit allows the creation of throwaway accounts, unlike other social media services. I neglected to mention that there is a proviso to that policy: "as long as you do not do so to ghost vote your own submissions".[23] In other words, do whatever you like, but don't interfere with the numbers. But in fact, the numbers are interfered with on every social media platform, provided your pockets are deep enough. As such, what is popular on Western social media may simply be what money can buy.

VALUING OUR SELVES

So, it is difficult to sustain the claim that social media data accurately represents human psychology, because so much of it is artificially inflated in several directions. But, more crucially, with all the censored content, fake accounts and inflated numbers, then how exactly can our behaviour on social media be authentic? Perhaps this is why 'profile work' is so exhausting – because we are in such an uncertain environment.

Naturally, the other side of that conundrum remains – whether or not social media influences psychology. By now, I am sure you can see how simplistic a question that seems in the face of such a complex phenomenon. We have seen differences between services, such as how Facebook and Snapchat differ with regard to social capital, and how Instagram and Flickr have distinct social networks. We also saw that changes in design have produced psychological consequences, such as the introduction of Facebook News Feeds and their transformation from chronologic to algorithmic ordering – moreover, within the broad features of social media (the fixity of our profiles, the cliques in our connections, the visibility of our updates and the permanency of the media we share), how multifaceted those effects must be. In addition, bearing in mind the many defunct services we encountered, juxtaposed with those services still functioning with many years of archived content, it is difficult to ascertain developmental effects.

Hence, a crucial aspect of social media psychology becomes how well we understand how these services work. In years to come it may well transpire that the upshot of current controversies is that we end up with smarter social media services and perhaps a deeper understanding of human psychology too, but we are a long way from that at present.

In today's technological societies, managing individuals does require dealing with using particular values. But in most cases those numbers are transparently calculated. Your age, credit rating, body-mass index, bank balance, exam scores, taxes – the crucial numbers that appraise the individual in a modern bureaucracy – are relatively transparent in how they are calculated. In contrast, how social media values us remains obscure.

Consequently, maybe the reason we sometimes feel disappointed by social media is because deep down we know, like Carmen Hermosillo did, that we are being used. And sure, a lot of the time social media is fun and enjoyable, but perhaps this is because, like many home truths, this reality of social media remains unspoken.

As has been suggested before, there is a kind of prisoner's dilemma at play in social media. If everyone resisted sharing their private information with these services, then they would have to find some way of operating without it. But because we seem to have a compelling desire to see each other's personal information, we divulge our own as part of a plea bargain. And this is the problem at the heart of the privacy paradox – we pursue personal self-interest by promoting ourselves on social media, while collectively our privacy would have been stronger had we not.

It is for this reason that I suspect that anti-social media boycotts like #deletefacebook or #DeactiDay will not come to much. Now that most people are on social media, it has a kind of monopoly effect, and so the sameness quality I mentioned at the start will probably continue as there are no viable alternatives on the horizon.

We all need to be a bit smarter about how we use these services, and not just those sending late night private messages. The technology that billions of us have incorporated into our everyday lives – multitasking across work and leisure – no one has ever had any training on how to use. That should change – it is clear that wider and more comprehensive digital education is warranted in many countries. Equally, policy makers must develop smarter regulation, which necessitates more interdisciplinary, critical and transparent research. Everyone has their part to play in making social media work better, and users must think carefully about how what they want from it. Crucially, the owners of these services must consider not so much how people use social media to connect with each other, but rather how each user uses their services to connect with themselves.

I neglected to mention at the start of this book how it began its life. Almost a decade ago, I started blogging on the psychology of Facebook. I was confident that Facebook would soon be defunct like Bebo and Friendster, and 'PsychBook Research' would be an interesting project for a year or two, and then I could move on to something else. Mercifully, I never put this prediction in print, but it is for that reason I am loath to commit to any forecasting on these topics.

However, as I did note in the first chapter, while social media is personal, like a diary or a self-help book, it is essentially a public transmission, like television or a newspaper. Much attention has focussed on the latter aspect of these services, but I hope in closing this book that you can appreciate that its future depends equally on understanding the former: the psychology of social media.

FURTHER READING

Beer, D. (2016). *Metric power*. London: Palgrave Macmillan.

boyd, danah. (2014). *It's complicated: The social lives of networked teens*. New Haven, CT: Yale University Press.

Danziger, K. (1997). *Naming the mind: How psychology found its language*. London: Sage.

De Vos, J. (2013). *Psychologization and the subject of late modernity*. London: Palgrave Macmillan.

Howard, P., & Wooley, S. (eds.) (2018). *Computational propaganda: Political parties, politicians, and political manipulation on social media*. Oxford: Oxford University Press.

Hughes, B. (2018). *Psychology in crisis*. London: Red Globe Press.

Livingstone, S., & Blum-Ross, A. (forthcoming). *Parenting for a digital future*. Oxford: Oxford University Press.

Marwick, A. E. (2013). *Status update: Celebrity, publicity and branding in the social media age*. New Haven, CT: Yale University Press.

Rainie, L., & Wellman, B. (2012). *Networked: The new social operating system*. Cambridge, MA: MIT Press.

Rose, N. (1989). *Governing the soul*. London: Free Association Books.

Suler, J. R. (2015). *Psychology of the digital age: Humans become electric*. Cambridge: Cambridge University Press.

Taylor, C. (1989). *Sources of the self: The making of modern identity*. Cambridge, MA: Harvard University Press.

Vaidhyanathan, S. (2018). *Antisocial media: How Facebook disconnects us and undermines democracy*. Oxford: Oxford University Press.

van Dijck, J. (2013). *The culture of connectivity: A critical history of social media*. Oxford: Oxford University Press.

NOTES

CHAPTER 1

1 Regarding plural/singular connotations, suffice it to say that I am talking about the social media *phenomenon* and its psychological aspects and effects, hence I am using it in the singular. When using it in a plural sense, I will specify further by using a phrase like 'social media services'.

2 "To alter information in a person's profile on a social networking website without his or her permission". From 'Frape' (2018). *Collins English dictionary*. Retrieved from www.collinsdictionary.com/dictionary/english/frape

3 "Fear Of Missing Out". From 'FOMO' (2018). *Collins English dictionary*. Retrieved from www.collinsdictionary.com/dictionary/english/fomo

CHAPTER 2

1 The blog is still online at http://damascusgaygirl.blogspot.com/, though most of the posts have been removed. However, some have been preserved at various archives around the internet.

2 Arraf, A. (2011, April 26). My father, the hero. *A Gay Girl in Damascus*. Retrieved from Library of Congress Web Archive http://webarchive.loc.gov/all/20110428090825/http://damascusgaygirl.blogspot.com/2011/04/my-father-hero.html

3 Wilson, J. (2011, May 10). A gay girl in Damascus: Lesbian blogger becomes Syrian hero. *TIME*. Retrieved from http://newsfeed.time.com/2011/05/10/a-gay-girl-in-damascus-lesbian-blogger-becomes-syrian-hero/

4 Marsh, K. (2011, May 6). A gay girl in Damascus becomes a heroine of the Syrian revolt. *The Guardian*. Retrieved from www.theguardian.com/world/2011/may/06/gay-girl-damascus-syria-blog

5 Flock, E. (2011, June 7). 'Gay Girl in Damascus' Syrian blogger allegedly kidnapped. *The Washington Post*. Retrieved from www.washingtonpost.com/blogs/blogpost/post/gay-girl-in-damascus-syrian-blogger-allegedly-kidnapped/2011/06/07/AGIhp1KH_blog.html

6 McDermott, S. (2011, June 8). From the web team – Newsnight. *BBC News*. Retrieved from www.bbc.co.uk/blogs/newsnight/fromthewebteam/2011/06/wednesday_8_june_2011.html

7 Bell, M., & Flock, E. (2011, June 12). 'A Gay Girl in Damascus' comes clean. *The Washington Post*. Retrieved from www.washingtonpost.com/lifestyle/style/a-gay-girl-in-damascus-comes-clean/2011/06/12/AGkyH0RH_story.html

8 Carvin, A. [@acarvin] (2011, June 6). *Dear god – she's been kidnapped? RT @MalathAumran:Amina Abdallah: Please read the latest post on her blog* http://j.mp/j5L2dZ #Syria. Retrieved from https://twitter.com/acarvin/status/77804332778659841

9 Flock, E., & Bell, M. (2011, June 13). Tom MacMaster, the man behind 'A Gay Girl in Damascus:' 'I didn't expect the story to get so big'. *The Washington Post*. Retrieved from www.washingtonpost.com/blogs/blogpost/post/tom-macmaster-the-man-behind-a-gay-girl-in-damascus-i-didnt-expect-the-story-to-get-so-big/2011/06/13/AGhnHiSH_blog.html

10 MacMaster, T. (2011, June 13). Apology to readers. *A Gay Girl in Damascus*. Retrieved from Internet Archive's Wayback Machine https://web.archive.org/web/20110613222309/http://damascusgaygirl.blogspot.com/

11 Marwick, A. (2005, October 5–9). I'm more than just a Friendster profile: Identity, authenticity, and power in social networking services. *Association for Internet Researchers 6.0*.

12 Oser, K. (2004, July 21). Friendster Courts Hollywood. *Ad Age*. New York. Retrieved from http://adage.com/article/madisonvine-case-study/friendster-courts-hollywood/40663/

13 Zhao, S., Grasmuck, S., & Martin, J. (2008). Identity construction on Facebook: Digital empowerment in anchored relationships. *Computers in Human Behavior*, 24(5), 1816–1836. https://doi.org/10.1016/j.chb.2008.02.012

14 Uski, S., & Lampinen, A. (2016). Social norms and self-presentation on social network sites: Profile work in action. *New Media & Society*, 18(3), 447–464. https://doi.org/10.1177/1461444814543164

15 Barnes, S. B. (2006). A privacy paradox: Social networking in the United States. *First Monday*, 11(9), 5. https://doi.org/10.5210/fm.v11i9.1394

16 Leavitt, A. (2015). "This is a Throwaway Account": Temporary technical identities and perceptions of anonymity in a massive online community. In *Proceedings of the 18th ACM conference on computer supported cooperative work & social computing* (pp. 317–327). New York: ACM Press. https://doi.org/10.1145/2675133.2675175

17 Reddit. (2018). *Frequently asked questions*. Retrieved from www.reddit.com/r/%20reddit.com/wiki/faq

18 Moncur, W., Orzech, K. M., & Neville, F. G. (2016). Fraping, social norms and online representations of self. *Computers in Human Behavior*, 63, 125–131. https://doi.org/10.1016/j.chb.2016.05.042

19 Bernstein, M. S., Monroy-Hernández, A., Harry, D., André, P., Panovich, K., & Vargas, G. (2011). 4chan and/b: An analysis of anonymity and ephemerality in a large online community. In *International AAAI Conference on Web and Social Media* (pp. 50–57). Menlo Park, CA: AAAI Press.

CHAPTER 3

1 Levin, J. (2014, August 22). Who invented the ice bucket challenge? *Slate*. Retrieved from www.slate.com/articles/technology/technology/2014/08/who_invented_the_ice_bucket_challenge_a_slate_investigation.single.html

2 Sifferlin, A. (2014, August 18). Here's how the ALS ice bucket challenge actually started. *TIME*. Retrieved from http://time.com/3136507/als-ice-bucket-challenge-started/

3 van Ogtrop, K. (n.d.). Ever wonder how the whole "Ice Bucket Challenge" started? *Real Simple*. Retrieved from www.realsimple.com/magazine-more/jeanette-senerchia-ice-bucket

4 Facebook. (2014, August 18). The ice bucket challenge on Facebook. *Facebook Newsroom*. Retrieved from https://newsroom.fb.com/news/2014/08/the-ice-bucket-challenge-on-facebook/

5 Woolf, N. (2016, July 27). Remember the ice bucket challenge? It just funded an ALS breakthrough. *The Guardian*. Retrieved from www.theguardian.com/society/2016/jul/26/ice-bucket-challenge-als-charity-gene-discovery

6 Ellison, N. B., Steinfield, C., & Lampe, C. (2007). The benefits of Facebook "Friends": Social capital and college students' use of online social network sites. *Journal of Computer-Mediated Communication*, 12(4), 1143–1168. https://doi.org/10.1111/j.1083-6101.2007.00367.x

7 Piwek, L., & Joinson, A. (2016). "What do they snapchat about?" Patterns of use in time-limited instant messaging service. *Computers in Human Behavior*, 54, 358–367. https://doi.org/10.1016/j.chb.2015.08.026

8 Foley, M. (2016, May 24). What is a Snapchat streak? Here's everything you need to know about Snapstreaks. *Bustle*. Retrieved from www.bustle.com/articles/162803-what-is-a-snapchat-streak-heres-everything-you-need-to-know-about-snapstreaks

9 Dunbar, R. I. M. (1992). Neocortex size as a constraint on group size in primates. *Journal of Human Evolution*, 22(6), 469–493. https://doi.org/10.1016/0047-2484(92)90081-J

10 Dunbar, R. I. M. (2016). Do online social media cut through the constraints that limit the size of offline social networks? *Royal Society Open Science*, 3(1), 1–9. https://doi.org/10.1098/rsos.150292

11 Marwick, A. E., & boyd, danah. (2010). I tweet honestly, I tweet passionately: Twitter users, context collapse, and the imagined audience. *New Media & Society*, 13(1), 114–133. https://doi.org/10.1177/1461444810365313

12 Festl, R., & Quandt, T. (2013). Social relations and cyberbullying: The influence of individual and structural attributes on victimization and perpetration via the internet. *Human Communication Research*, 39(1), 101–126. https://doi.org/10.1111/j.1468-2958.2012.01442.x

13 Przybylski, A. K., Murayama, K., Dehaan, C. R., & Gladwell, V. (2013). Motivational, emotional, and behavioral correlates of fear of missing out. *Computers in Human Behavior*, 29(4), 1841–1848. https://doi.org/10.1016/j.chb.2013.02.014

CHAPTER 4

1 Bowcott, O. (2012, July 27). Twitter joke trial: Paul Chambers wins high court appeal against conviction. *The Guardian*. Retrieved from www.theguardian.com/law/2012/jul/27/twitter-joke-trial-high-court

2 Chambers' tweet has evidently been deleted but has been reproduced in many news reports, including those cited here.

3 Chambers, P. (2010, May 11). My tweet was silly, but the police reaction was absurd. *The Guardian*. Retrieved from www.theguardian.com/commentisfree/libertycentral/2010/may/11/tweet-joke-criminal-record-airport

4 Doughty, S. (2012, July 27). Accountant wins appeal against conviction for airport bomb Tweet after judge realises it was a JOKE. *The Daily Mail*. Retrieved from www.dailymail.co.uk/news/article-2179782/Twitter-joke-trial-Paul-Chambers-wins-appeal-conviction-airport-bomb-Tweet.html

5 Archer, B. (2017, July 28). 'Twitter joke' trial brought fairytale ending for Co Down woman. *The Irish News*. Retrieved from www.irishnews.com/news/2017/07/28/news/-twitter-joke-trial-brought-fairytale-ending-for-co-down-woman-1095302/

6 Suler, J. (2004). The online disinhibition effect. *CyberPsychology & Behavior*, 7(3), 321–326. https://doi.org/10.1089/1094931041291295

7 Hoadley, C. M., Xu, H., Lee, J. J., & Rosson, M. B. (2010). Privacy as information access and illusory control: The case of the Facebook News Feed privacy outcry. *Electronic Commerce Research and Applications*, 9(1), 50–60. https://doi.org/10.1016/j.elerap.2009.05.001

8 Debatin, B., Lovejoy, J. P., Horn, A-K., & Hughes, B. N. (2009). Facebook and online privacy: Attitudes, behaviors, and unintended consequences. *Journal of Computer-Mediated Communication*, 15(1), 83–108. https://doi.org/10.1111/j.1083-6101.2009.01494.x

9 Bucher, T. (2012). Want to be on the top? Algorithmic power and the threat of invisibility on Facebook. *New Media & Society*, 14(7), 1164–1180. https://doi.org/10.1177/1461444812440159

10 Instagram. (n.d.). Feed. *Instagram Help Center*. Retrieved from https://help.instagram.com/1986234648360433/

11 LinkedIn. (n.d.). Visibility and impact of your social activity on the LinkedIn feed. *LinkedIn Help*. Retrieved from www.linkedin.com/help/linkedin/answer/85598

12 Twitter. (n.d.). About your Twitter timeline. *Twitter Help Center*. Retrieved from https://help.twitter.com/en/using-twitter/twitter-timeline#settings

13 Bauer, L., Cranor, L. F., Komanduri, S., Mazurek, M. L., Reiter, M. K., Sleeper, M., & Ur, B. (2013). The post anachronism: The temporal dimension of Facebook privacy. In *Proceedings of the 12th ACM workshop on workshop on privacy in the electronic society* (pp. 1–12). New York: ACM Press. https://doi.org/10.1145/2517840.2517859

14 Brandtzaeg, P. B., & Lüders, M. (2018). Time collapse in social media: Extending the context collapse. *Social Media + Society*, 4(1), 205630511876334. https://doi.org/10.1177/2056305118763349

CHAPTER 5

1 Stern, M. (2014, October 13). 'The Snappening' is real: 90,000 private photos and 9,000 hacked Snapchat videos leak online. *The Daily Beast*. Retrieved from www.thedailybeast.com/articles/2014/10/13/the-snappening-is-real-90k-private-photos-and-9k-videos-hacked-and-leaked-online.html

2 Kamps, H. J. (2016, March 15). Prosecutors find that 'Fappening' celebrity nudes leak was not Apple's fault. *TechCrunch*. Retrieved from https://techcrunch.com/2016/03/15/prosecutors-find-that-fappening-celebrity-nudes-leak-was-not-apples-fault/

3 Tufft, B. (2014, October 12). The Snappening: What is 4chan's latest scandal – and is the Snapchat 'leak' a hoax? *The Independent*. Retrieved from www.independent.co.uk/incoming/the-snappening-what-is-4chans-latest-scandal-and-is-it-really-a-hoax-9789389.html

4 Gilbert, B. (2014, October 10). Snapchat servers 'were never breached,' but your snaps may still be compromised (update). *Engadget*. Retrieved from www.engadget.com/2014/10/10/snapchat-snapsave-alleged-breach/

5 Vincent, J. (2014, October 13). Has Snapchat been hacked? What's SnapSaved? Your questions answered. *The Independent*. Retrieved from www.independent.co.uk/life-style/gadgets-and-tech/the-snappening-has-snapchat-been-hacked-whats-snapsaved-your-questions-answered-9790658.html

6 Lombard, M. & Ditton, T. (1997). At the heart of it all: The concept of presence. *Journal of Computer-Mediated Communication*, 3(2), 1–23. https://doi.org/10.1111/j.1083-6101.1997.tb00072.x

7 Manikonda, L., Hu, Y., & Kambhampati, S. (2014). *Analyzing user activities, demographics, social network structure and user-generated content on Instagram*. Retrieved from http://arxiv.org/abs/1410.8099

8 Tang, J. C., Venolia, G., & Inkpen, K. M. (2016). Meerkat and Periscope. In *Proceedings of the 2016 CHI conference on human factors in computing systems* (pp. 4770–4780). New York: ACM Press. https://doi.org/10.1145/2858036.2858374

9 Tang et al., (2016), p. 4777.

10 Mlot, S. (2016, October 3). Streaming app Meerkat is officially dead. *PC Mag*. Retrieved from www.pcmag.com/news/348393/streaming-app-meerkat-is-officially-dead

11 Schwarz, O. (2010). On friendship, boobs and the logic of the catalogue: Online self-portraits as a means for the exchange of capital. *Convergence: The International Journal of Research into New Media Technologies*, 16(2), 163–183. https://doi.org/10.1177/1354856509357582
12 Soha, M., & McDowell, Z. J. (2016). Monetizing a meme: YouTube, Content ID, and the Harlem Shake. *Social Media + Society*, 2(1), 1–12. https://doi.org/10.1177/2056305115623801
13 Wagner, K. (2017, April 27). Facebook will let video creators make money when people pirate their videos. *Recode*. Retrieved from www.recode.net/2017/4/27/15459204/facebook-video-rights-revenue-pirate

CHAPTER 6

1 Jacobson, M. (2009, May 3). Anthony and the giant. *New York Magazine*. Retrieved from http://nymag.com/news/politics/56440/
2 Cordova, G. N. (2011, June 2). My statement on Anthony Weiner and the lewd photo tweet. *The Guardian*. Retrieved from www.theguardian.com/commentisfree/cifamerica/2011/jun/02/twitter-photo-anthony-weiner
3 Parker, A., & Barbaro, M. (2011, June 8). In reckless fashion, rapid online pursuits of political admirers. *The New York Times*. Retrieved from www.nytimes.com/2011/06/09/nyregion/weiners-pattern-turning-political-admirers-into-online-pursuits.html
4 Salvatore, P. J. (2011, May 28). Weinergate: Congressman claims "Facebook Hacked" as lewd photo hits Twitter. *Breitbart*. Retrieved from www.breitbart.com/big-journalism/2011/05/28/weinergate-congressman-claims-facebook-hacked-as-lewd-photo-hits-twitter-2/
5 Ehrlich, B. (2011, June 3). Yfrog says it wasn't compromised in wake of Weiner photo. *Mashable*. Retrieved from https://mashable.com/2011/06/03/yfrog-email-upload/
6 Dorsey, J. (2011, June 1). search+photos. *Twitter Blog*. Retrieved from https://blog.twitter.com/official/en_us/a/2011/searchphotos.html
7 Casarez, J. (2017, November 6). Anthony Weiner reports to prison. CNN. Retrieved from https://edition.cnn.com/2017/11/06/us/weiner-reports-to-prison/index.html
8 Walther, J. B. (2007). Selective self-presentation in computer-mediated communication: Hyperpersonal dimensions of technology, language, and cognition. *Computers in Human Behavior*, 23(5), 2538–2557. https://doi.org/10.1016/j.chb.2006.05.002

9 Golder, S. A., Wilkinson, D. M., & Huberman, B. A. (2007). Rhythms of social interaction: Messaging within a massive online network. In *Communities and technologies 2007* (pp. 41–66). London: Springer. https://doi.org/10.1007/978-1-84628-905-7_3

10 NB average of 180 as in mean, though with a median of 144 – a disparity due to a small number of users having a very large number of friends.

11 Utz, S. (2015). The function of self-disclosure on social network sites: Not only intimate, but also positive and entertaining self-disclosures increase the feeling of connection. *Computers in Human Behavior*, 45, 1–10. https://doi.org/10.1016/j.chb.2014.11.076

12 Edwards, A., & Harris, C. J. (2016, August). To tweet or 'subtweet'? Impacts of social networking post directness and valence on interpersonal impressions. *Computers in Human Behavior*, 63, 304–310. https://doi.org/10.1016/j.chb.2016.05.050

13 Gan, C., & Wang, W. (2015). Uses and gratifications of social media: A comparison of microblog and WeChat. *Journal of Systems and Information Technology*, 17(4), 351–363. https://doi.org/10.1108/JSIT-06-2015-0052

14 Simon, T., Goldberg, A., Leykin, D., & Adini, B. (2016). Kidnapping WhatsApp – rumors during the search and rescue operation of three kidnapped youth. *Computers in Human Behavior*, 64, 183–190. https://doi.org/10.1016/j.chb.2016.06.058

CHAPTER 7

1 Meaning 'too long, didn't read'. From 'tl; dr' (2018). *Collins English dictionary*. Retrieved from www.collinsdictionary.com/dictionary/english/tl-dr

2 Although not officially recorded as a suicide, those close to her have called her death a 'passive suicide' in that she seems to have stopped taking critical medication prior to her death. See Meadows, M. S., & Ludlow, P. (2009, September 2). A virtual life: An actual death. *h+ Magazine*. Retrieved from http://hplusmagazine.com/2009/09/02/virtual-life-actual-death/

3 Well.com. (n.d.). What is The WELL? *The WELL*. Emeryville CA: The Well Group, Inc. Retrieved from https://www.well.com/about-2/.

4 Well.com. (n.d.).

5 Rheingold, H. (1993). *The virtual community: Homesteading on the electronic frontier*. Reading, MA: Addison-Wesley.

6 Turner, F. (2005). Where the counterculture met the new economy: The WELL and the origins of virtual community. *Technology and Culture*, 46(3), 485–512. https://doi.org/10.1353/tech.2005.0154

7 This was the tagline on the Facebook's homepage from about 2008 until about 2012 (see https://web.archive.org/web/20081226230545/www.facebook.com/ and https://web.archive.org/web/20121231135906/www.facebook.com/).

8 Humdog. (1996). Pandora's vox: On community in cyberspace. In P. Ludlow (Ed.), *High noon on the electronic frontier: Conceptual issues in cyberspace* (pp. 437–444). Cambridge, MA: MIT Press.

9 Carmen Hermosillo. (n.d.). [LinkedIn profile page] Retrieved from www.linkedin.com/in/carmen-hermosillo-373a303/

10 Cadwalladr, C., & Graham-Harrison, E. (2018, March 25). How Cambridge Analytica turned Facebook 'likes' into a lucrative political tool. *The Guardian*. Retrieved from www.theguardian.com/technology/2018/mar/17/facebook-cambridge-analytica-kogan-data-algorithm

11 Kosinski, M., Stillwell, D., & Graepel, T. (2013). Private traits and attributes are predictable from digital records of human behavior. *Proceedings of the National Academy of Sciences of the United States of America*, 110(15), 5802–5805. https://doi.org/10.1073/pnas.1218772110

12 Borns, J. (2015, September 21). What's your Zodiac sign's ice cream flavor? *Buzzfeed*. Retrieved from www.buzzfeed.com/joannaborns/ice-cream-flavor-zodiac-sign

13 Michonneau, P., & Padjemi, J. (2018, June 8). We know how many sexual partners you've had based on your favorite potato dish. *Buzzfeed*. Retrieved from www.buzzfeed.com/bullo/the-potato-knows-all

14 The Psychometrics Centre. (n.d.). *MyPersonality database*. Cambridge Judge Business School, University of Cambridge. Retrieved from www.psychometrics.cam.ac.uk/productsservices/mypersonality

15 Cellan-Jones, R. (2018, April 24). Facebook explored unpicking personalities to target ads. *BBC News*. Retrieved www.bbc.com/news/technology-43869911

16 Eckles, D., Gordon, B. R., & Johnson, G. A. (2018). Field studies of psychologically targeted ads face threats to internal validity. *Proceedings of the National Academy of Sciences*, 1(C), 201805363. https://doi.org/10.1073/pnas.1805363115

17 Donchenko, D., Ovchar, N., Sadovnikova, N., Parygin, D., Shabalina, O., & Ather, D. (2017). Analysis of comments of users of social networks to assess

the level of social tension. *Procedia Computer Science*, 119, 359–367. https://doi.org/10.1016/j.procs.2017.11.195

18 van Dijck, J. (2014). Datafication, dataism and dataveillance: Big Data between scientific paradigm and ideology. *Surveillance & Society*, 12(2), 197–208. https://doi.org/10.24908/ss.v12i2.4776

19 Wagner, K., & Molla, R. (2018, May 15). Facebook has disabled almost 1.3 billion fake accounts over the past six months. *Recode*. Retrieved from www.recode.net/2018/5/15/17349790/facebook-mark-zuckerberg-fake-accounts-content-policy-update

20 Timberg, C., & Dwoskin, E. (2018, July 6). Twitter is sweeping out fake accounts like never before, putting user growth at risk. *The Washington Post*. Retrieved from www.washingtonpost.com/technology/2018/07/06/twitter-is-sweeping-out-fake-accounts-like-never-before-putting-user-growth-risk/

21 Bamman, D., O'Connor, B., & Smith, N. (2012). Censorship and deletion practices in Chinese social media. *First Monday*, 17(3). https://doi.org/10.5210/fm.v17i3.3943

22 Héder, M. (2018). A black market for upvotes and likes. Retrieved from http://arxiv.org/abs/1803.07029

23 Reddit. (2018). Frequently asked questions. *Reddit*. Retrieved from www.reddit.com/r/%20reddit.com/wiki/faq

9781138047754